Into the Dragon's Teeth

Warriors' Tales of the Battle of the Bulge

Into the Dragon's Teeth

Warriors' Tales of the Battle of the Bulge

Dan Lynch
&
Paul Rutherford

Whitston Publishing Company, Inc.
Albany, New York
2006

Library of Congress Control Number 2003114119

ISBN 0-87875-559-4

Printed in the United States of America

Photos and maps courtesy of the
Times Union, Albany, N.Y.,
Richard Marowitz, Al Cohen and Doug Vink.

*To Jim Lynch—and to the memories of Jerry Lynch and
John (Chunky) Lynch—and to all those who stood
so tall in so terrible a time.*

INTRODUCTION

☆ ☆

In 1944, America struck back.

Reeling from the surprise attack on Pearl Harbor that had plunged an unwary nation into the second mammoth war of the 20th Century, the United States had been on the defensive for several years. General Douglas MacArthur, the Pacific military commander, had fled his headquarters in the Philippines in a PT boat and retreated to Australia to mount a counteroffensive. In Europe, the Third Reich's ruthlessly efficient war machine had plowed through the Continent, conquering France with ease, and was slaughtering British civilians with murderous air raids on teeming cities and bucolic towns. The heel of Adolf Hitler's boot was squarely on the planet's neck.

All that changed on June 6, 1944. After several years of transforming America's industrial plant to produce weaponry on a grand scale—and with a renewed, vengeful MacArthur sweeping through the Pacific toward Japan—the United States and its allies crossed the English Channel in the greatest armada the world had ever seen to invade the European mainland at Normandy. The D-Day invasion represented the most monumental movement of men and war materiel in human history. Once the beachhead was established in a tidal wave of blood, the U.S. and its allies began pushing the Germans back from their conquests—back toward the Fatherland.

As the weather cooled and Europe fell into the grip of the most bitter winter in decades, American boys who'd been drafted into military service hastily finished up training and were shipped overseas to replace the men who'd perished on Normandy's beaches. The new soldiers were mostly teenagers for whom shaving was still an adventure. Bright-eyed and unsure of what lay ahead, they arrived in Europe and settled into their units for the final push into Germany.

Then the Germans struck back.

On December 16th, Hitler unleashed a ferocious counterattack that took the Allies totally by surprise. It remains unclear why Allied intelligence had failed to pick up advance indications of the counteroffensive, but that was a matter of only minor significance to the American soldiers in the field. Suddenly, they found themselves swept up in what was dubbed the Battle of the Bulge—the most momentous military engagement of the mechanized age. As a uniquely cruel winter sank its icy fangs into northern Europe, a million or more men were locked in mortal combat on a battlefield that ranged over much of a continent. The U.S. forces consisted of battle-hardened survivors of D-Day and untested replacements fresh from an America still scarred by the Great Depression. In the end, at huge personal sacrifice and in what was to become the proudest moment of their lives, they ultimately broke the back of the Nazi war machine.

This is the story of three of those men. For the most part, their stories are less unique than typical. They are the stories of many members of the U.S. Army in the closing months of the War in Europe and during the months of occupation that followed. They are stories gleaned from many hours of intense personal interviews with the men as individuals and in a group, where the recollections of one man often stirred recollections by the others. These interviews were conducted over several months during the late winter and spring of 2003, nearly six full decades after many of the events occurred. In some cases, the story of a particular incident was gone over time after time with the goal of removing from the recitation any hint of confusion or inconsistency.

Some of these memories were painful for the men

who'd lived through the events, had overcome the horror of their experiences and moved on to new, less trying adventures in life. This is the story of each man, as he best recalls it and as best the facts can be determined over the course of those lengthy interviews. In some cases, details like names and precise places were lost in the shroud of time. In others, fresh insights emerged under questioning. Each man recalled the experience as a series of isolated episodes strung together against a larger tapestry of a world at war.

The men were aided in their recollections by their own records of their time as warriors, by events recorded in their unit histories and by the memories of those close to them. Each man also had the opportunity to go over the recitation of these warriors' tales before this book was printed. In short, what you will read here is the best available version of truth as recounted almost a lifetime later by three of the gallant, gutsy guys who saved the world from the most towering evil since Genghis Khan.

☆ ☆ ☆ ☆ ☆

It's just after lunch, and they're moving into the auditorium—not quite a hundred of them. They're high school students in jeans and Tommy Hilfiger sweatshirts. Carrying books, chatting and laughing, they take their seats. Down in front, at the bottom of the descending rows of theater-style seats, sit three elderly men in outdated olive drab military uniforms. They're facing the students from behind a long table. Arrayed across the front of the table, facing the students, is a vast Nazi flag—a sea of blood red with a white circle in the center in which is displayed a twisted cross of black. Atop the flag stretched across the tabletop are maps, photographs, samples of military equipment issued to soldiers in an earlier time and, incongruously, a badly battered silk top hat.

Niskayuna High School serves an upscale community several miles northwest of Albany, N.Y. It's generally considered one of the best of the suburban high schools in the Albany metro area. That's largely because it draws so many of its students from the homes of well-educated professionals, many of whom work at reasonably high levels in New York state government. Or the parents are highly trained employees of General Electric in sophisticated technical research facilities in the area. In general, Niskayuna High School students live comfortable lives. They enjoy the best of what early 21st Century America has to offer young people from relatively prosperous families. On this crisp, sun-splashed, winter day, they are about to learn what life served up to members of an earlier generation who, at roughly the same stage in life, were living vastly different lives.

Warriors are members of a unique society. They know things that others do not know. They have endured triumphs, travails and tragedies that are essentially incomprehensible to those who have not suffered through the harrowing, soul-searing experience of combat. As they banded together on the battlefield, so do warriors tend to band together in the life that follows—in veterans groups, in parades, at funerals. They tend not to discuss their experiences with those who have not shared them—with people who have not seen what they saw, done what they've done, felt what they've felt or had inflicted upon them both the horrors of warfare and the demons of memory.

World War II veterans in particular have been a close-mouthed lot in the decades since V-E Day and V-J Day. For the most part, they went to war as children and returned home as men—sadder and wiser and uniquely equipped to put the horror behind them and to build the brawniest economy the world has ever known. It is only now, as the surviving warriors of World War II are dying off at a rate of 1,000 a day, that some of these gallant old men are breaking a lifetime's silence. For some of this remarkable, vanishing generation, it's important to at last share their special understanding of how ugly life can be—and how precious it is—and what it can demand of those confronted by challenges that cannot be ignored.

As the group quiets, a teacher introduces the three. Doug Vink is the first to rise. Smallish, white-haired, bespectacled and wiry, he picks up a hand microphone attached to the auditorium's sound system. To his right, Richard Marowitz and Al Cohen sit quietly. These three septuagenarians have done this before. For several years, they've been visiting schools as varied as thriving Niskayuna and Tryon, a state-run school for juvenile criminals, to explain what life was like when they were young. The world of their youth was a profoundly unlovely place, and what Vink, Marowitz and Cohen did in those years paved the way for the security and comforts enjoyed nearly six decades later by these kids in their sleek suburban high school. Vink, Marowitz and Cohen were in the thick of terrible times, and they want these young people to understand what they might, at some point, be called upon to endure themselves.

"The reason I'm first," Doug Vink says into the microphone, "is that I'm the youngest, and I'm the best-looking one of the group."

A titter of laughter runs through the assembled students. The microphone in his left hand, Vink paces back and forth behind the table.

"It would be unfair for me," Vink says, "to take you people right now and drop you right in the middle of the Bulge. So, I'll back up to a month before."

He then gives the students a brief overview of the events leading up to the Battle of the Bulge—of the immense bloodshed on both sides after Allied troops landed at Normandy, of the fierce combat that led the Allied brass to mistakenly conclude that the German army was finished, of the terrified French refugees who later flooded to Allied lines with stories of huge Nazi armies massing to the north—refugees who simply hadn't been believed.

And then, Vink tells the students, just before Christmas, the Germans spit out their answer to the Allied invasion. In massive force, they counterattacked with an intensity that no one had expected. They tore into the Allied forces with the hard-eyed resolve of desperate men who knew that only they stood between the invading enemy troops and their beloved homeland. The Germans stopped backing up. Instead, they charged forward, and the Allies were driven back. The Battle of the Bulge was in full swing in a clash to the death in waist-deep snow.

"They had the best equipment," Doug Vink tells the students solemnly, "the greatest equipment. And I will tell you right now, and these other two fellows will probably agree with me, don't underestimate what the German army had during World War II. They were better equipped and better trained and more disciplined than we were. We went like idiots because we were told to do it. We didn't know any better. . . ."

Fascists on the march
(*Associated Press Photo*)

THE WINDS OF WAR

> "People do not have the natural herd
> instinct . . . only fear of authority command-
> ing and using force can create a commu-
> nity."　　**—Adolf Hitler,** *Mein Kampf*

It was glorified by politicians as "The War to End All
Wars," but dark clouds hovered over Europe at the end of
World War I. After the bloodiest conflict the world had ever
known—more than 12 million dead, more than half of them
civilians—an uneasy, unsatisfying peace had been achieved.
The terms of the settlement, however, had sown the seeds of a
second worldwide conflict rooted in even deeper resentments
than the first. For all their self-congratulations, the politicians
had failed. Somewhere down the road, the generals would get
a second chance —and with vastly deadlier weaponry.

German generals had failed in what the world then
knew as The Great War. Despite overwhelming victory by the
Germans on the Eastern front against the Russians, the arrival
of American doughboys to bolster the British and French
armies had turned the tide on the Western Front and driven the
Germans from France. Germany had been forced to give up all
captured territories, pay damages to its opponents and agree to
a massive reduction of its armed forces, as mapped out by
President Woodrow Wilson in the Treaty of Versailles. This 14-
point peace document had not been received well by Germany
or the allies, France and Britain, since it effectively called for

the end of conquest of weaker nations, which had been standard practice in Europe since the creation of the nation-state.

The day the armistice was announced in 1918, a 29-year-old soldier who'd fought for the Kaiser was recovering in a hospital from temporary blindness caused by British mustard gas. Before the war he'd been a chronic underachiever, supposedly eager to study art or architecture but working instead as a day laborer in abject poverty, selling picture post cards and doing odd jobs to make ends meet. He'd fought bravely in the Great War, however, and was profoundly dismayed by the Fatherland's surrender. As he lay in bed, his eyes gradually regaining their focus, Adolf Hitler silently vowed to return Germany to its former greatness.

An Austrian who'd settled in Munich in 1913, Hitler decided after the war to pursue a political career. He joined a local army organization and was assigned to spy on the German Workers Party, which had only about two dozen members. Attending a party meeting and finding himself incensed by one of the speakers, Hitler rose and delivered a fiery rebuttal that so impressed the group's leader, Anton Drexler; that Hitler was invited to join the fledgling organization. After some thought, Hitler agreed. He quickly became a key figure in shaping and expanding the German Workers Party. Two years later, he founded the National Socialist German Workers Party—or, as it came to be nicknamed, the Nazi Party. The party's platform rested on three legs—hatred of the Treaty of Versailles, hatred of communists and hatred of Jews, whom Hitler blamed for polluting Germany's "racial purity."

By 1923, the Nazis had attracted as members some prominent veterans of the Great War—among them a full field marshal and Hermann Goering, a noted air combat ace. The Nazis also had established their own military organization, the Storm Troopers. An attempt to take over the City of Munich, however, failed when the National Guard opened fire. Fourteen Nazis were killed, and Hitler fled. Captured, put on trial and sentenced to five years in prison for treason, Hitler ended up serving less than a year—long enough to hammer his "German Master Race" doctrine into a book, *Mein Kampf* (My Struggle). Upon his release, Hitler was delighted to discover that his trial and incarceration had made him a celebrity. Despite a government ban against Nazi newspapers or any public speaking by Nazi leaders; the party began to gain ground as the established German government faltered.

In 1929, the world plunged into an economic depression. Germany was hit particularly hard. Millions of Germans were unemployed and in quest both of scapegoats and strong national leadership. By now, Hitler had become a German citizen. He ran for president and lost, but his Nazi Party was left as Germany's strongest, setting the stage in 1933 for Hitler to be named chancellor, the second most powerful position in the government. Later in the year, the Reichstag, the German national legislative building, burned to the ground. Communists did it, Hitler charged—although it had been Nazis who'd set the fire. Responding to what Hitler insisted was a national emergency, Germany's lawmakers promptly voted to grant the new chancellor dictatorial powers. In August 1934, after the death of President Paul von Hindenburg, Hitler succeeded him as president and took the new title of Fuhrer, or leader. In a few short years, Germany had been transformed into a totalitarian police state with a virulent animosity toward Jews.

Over the next three years Hitler went about with the "Nazification" of Germany. He was bent on breaking the Versailles Treaty and its strict limitations on the capability of the German army, navy and air force. In utmost secrecy, he ordered the armed forces tripled in size. The press, films, art and radio fell victim to extreme censorship as all youth groups were abolished and reformed into a single "Hitler Youth" entity. Churches that opposed his doctrine were persecuted and their clerics often arrested and sent to concentration camps.

Hitler believed that invaders had polluted the German bloodline and that Germany was obligated to conquer the world to cleanse it of the "lesser races"—of anyone not Nordic or Aryan. The Nuremberg Laws of 1935 reflected that philosophy by withdrawing German citizenship from Jews. No Jew could hold public office, vote, work in civil service, the media, farming, teaching, the stock exchange or, eventually, in the fields of law or medicine. Hostility toward Jews was encouraged. They became increasingly persecuted and ostracized in German society.

In defiance of the Versailles Treaty, Hitler ordered his naval chief, Admiral Erich Raeder, to construct warships vastly larger than permitted under the agreement and a fleet of submarines—vessels that also had been strictly forbidden. Goering, chief of the air force, was ordered to build the Luftwaffe into a fierce fighting force. In 1935, Hitler purposely leaked to British officials the existence of the banned aircraft—which, it was later learned, had already been known to them—to determine if the treaty would indeed be enforced. The reaction of France and England was to essentially ignore Germany's military buildup. That encouraged Hitler to openly engage in military induction, increasing German's army to approximately half a million men. Meanwhile, the Fuhrer was delivering spirited speeches denouncing war and stressing his desire for peace with his country's neighbors.

In March 1936, Hitler again tested the resolve of the allies to enforce the Versailles Treaty by marching German soldiers over bridges into the previously demilitarized Rhineland. A much larger French army near the border did nothing in response to the violation of this area, west of the Rhine River. Cheered by that passive reaction, Hitler continued to solidify his military position by rapidly building defensive fortifications along the French and Belgian borders while, at the same time, offering to enter into non-aggression pacts with France and Belgium. The Rhineland occupation represented genuine peril for Central Europe. Countries like Austria and Czechoslovakia relied on intervention by the French in the event of a German invasion, and the French had taken no action in response to Hitler's move into the Rhineland. Seven months later, Hitler formed an alliance with the far right-wing

Italian dictator, Benito Mussolini. Known as the Rome-Berlin Axis, the pact included an agreement on a common foreign policy and mutual defense.

As he tested the resolve of the nations that had won the Great War to enforce the terms of its armistice, Hitler's popularity continued to grow inside Germany, strengthening his power over the nation's military leadership. The winds of war were being fanned by the failure of France and England to enforce the letter, or even the spirit, of the Treaty of Versailles. They were allowing Hitler to edge ever closer to his goal of securing additional "living space" for Germany—for the lands of other nations to be gobbled up for the growth of his German Master Race and the ultimate racial "purification" of the planet.

In 1938, Germany annexed Austria. The nations that had defeated Germany in the Great War responded by meeting with Hitler in Munich, listening to his demands and giving Germany part of Czechoslovakia in exchange for a promise that Nazi expansionism would be satisfied. The following year, Hitler negotiated a non-aggression pact with the Soviet Union and promptly sent German tank divisions rolling into Poland, where the outdated Polish army struggled futilely to oppose the deadly fighting machines from the backs of horses.

Two days after the Germans invaded Poland, Britain, France, Australia and New Zealand declared war on Germany, followed by Canada. For the next nine months, Germany continued to invade and defeat its neighbors—including Denmark, Norway, Holland, Luxembourg and Belgium. On June 14, 1940, the German army entered France, forcing one of the major peacekeeping entities of Europe to sign an armistice. On September 27, 1940, Japan joined Germany and as one of the Axis powers. By mid-1941, the Germans had conquered and were in control of most of their neighbors. With the British busy battling the Italians and Germans in North Africa, Hitler then turned his attention to the conquest of the Soviet Union, with its rich array of natural resources. On June 22, 1941, the German army invaded the Russian homeland in flagrant violation of the non-aggression pact Hitler had signed with Soviet leader Josef Stalin. From the Fuhrer's standpoint, the treaty had been no more than a stall tactic to prevent the Russians from interfering with his invasion of Poland.

The Russians later admitted the loss of 1,200 aircraft within the first nine hours of the attack. Within a week, 90 per cent of the Soviet Union's frontline strength had been vanquished. Over the next several months, the Germans took Minsk, Smolensk, Novogrod, Kiev, Kharkov, Kursk and Rostov. By October 1941, German troops were marching on Moscow. As the German Army took control of the town of Orel, German press chief Otto Dietrich declared to the world's leading newspapers, "For military purposes, Soviet Russia is done for. The British dream of a two-front war is dead."

German General Heinz Guderian was a military strategist and avid proponent of the "Blitzkrieg or Lightning War"— the phrase first coined by an American journalist in *Time Magazine* to describe the quick penetration and obliteration tactics employed during the 1939 invasion of Poland. He was a master of this method of tank warfare and in command of Operation *Barbarosa*, the code name for Hitler's invasion of the Soviet Union. Known for his disagreements with Hitler concerning military strategy, he wrote on October 6, 1941, that snow had begun falling on the invading German Army. Six days later, snow still fell. Russian roads were a sea of mud. By November, Guderian was reporting to Berlin severe cases of frostbite among his troops and complaining that no winter clothing had arrived to save his troops from freezing to death.

On November 25th, the Germans launched a full-blown attack on Moscow. By December 4th, General Guderian was reporting the halt of the Second Panzer Army's assault on the city. The temperature had fallen to 31 below zero, and the next morning was five degrees colder. The ill-prepared German troops were confronting what Napoleon's Grand Army had suffered 130 years earlier, when they'd been defeated not by the Russian army but by the bitter Russian winter.

On December 5th, after only 10 days into the assault on

Moscow, the German Army formally abandoned its attack. The Germans had been stopped everywhere along the 200-mile, semicircular front around Moscow. The following day, Russian General Georgi Zhukov secured the Soviet capital by unleashing on the invaders 100 divisions equipped and trained for harsh weather conditions. During the following weeks, the Germany army —denied by Hitler permission to retreat, as the German generals had recommended—was pushed back from Moscow.

A day after the German invasion on the Eastern front froze in place, another Axis power with similar ambitions of conquest would wake a sleeping giant and usher the most powerful nation in the world out of its isolationist pipe dream and into the conflict full force. At the time, Americans were ambivalent about the conflict in Europe. They clearly favored Britain and France over Hitler's Nazi Germany but were overwhelmingly opposed to the United States entering the war. By early 1940, as news of Hitler's army rolling over western Europe reached American shores, public opinion began to shift in favor of decisive action. Several grass roots lobbying organizations evolved—including the Committee to Defend America by Aiding the Allies, formed to promote "all aid short of war," and the America First Committee, which included famed aviator Charles A. Lindbergh and called for avoiding war even at the expense of an Axis victory.

Democratic President Franklin D. Roosevelt, while campaigning for an unprecedented third term, maneuvered for bipartisan support of a pro-Allied foreign policy by appointing two international-minded Republicans as secretary of war and secretary of the navy. Two months before the election, he decided to trade 50 aged American destroyers to the British for military bases in the Caribbean. Roosevelt's Republican presidential opponent, Wendell Willkie, publicly supported this transaction. While neither candidate called for direct intervention, Roosevelt's election in November 1940, paved the way for American support of the Allied war effort, a clear break from the nation's isolationist past.

In early 1940, Congress had considered cutting defense spending, but after the German invasion of France a multi-billion-dollar increase was passed. By June, Roosevelt had set up a National Defense Research Committee, which oversaw new weapon programs—including the Manhattan Project, which ultimately produced the atomic bomb. The third-term President was faced with the daunting prospect of enlarging the Navy, in order to fight a two-ocean war, and of properly arming a virtually weaponless U.S. Army that had begun maneuvers in August 1940, using broomsticks to simulate machine guns and rain pipes as make-believe mortars. Roosevelt's most controversial pre-war initiative was to impose a peacetime draft, the first in American history, to bolster the woefully inadequate army, which numbered only 500,000 men. At the time, Hitler's fighting forces numbered nearly eight million men armed with the newest, most effective weaponry on the planet. In September 1940, the House of Representatives passed the draft by a one-vote margin.

Other actions by the United States made clear that America was not truly neutral and was at least pondering entry into the war. In January 1941, Roosevelt announced the Lend-Lease Program designed to provide England with up to 50 per cent of U.S. military production in return for a promise of postwar repayment. The bill was ratified in March. In August, it was expanded to include war supplies to the beleaguered Russians.

In early 1941, the U.S. Atlantic fleet was reorganized in an effort to protect the flow of lend-lease supplies to Britain. Later that year, in cooperation with the Royal Navy, the U.S. Navy began assisting in the tracking of German submarines. In September, after the *USS Greer* was fired on by a German U-boat, President Roosevelt issued a shoot-to-kill order that initiated an undeclared naval war between the U.S. and Germany. A month later, the American destroyers *Kearney* and *Reuben James* were torpedoed in the North Atlantic.

It came as a complete surprise, therefore, that the United States ended up eyeball deep in the war not because of any action by the Germans in the Atlantic but because the U.S. government had imposed severe, crippling economic sanctions on the Japanese Empire in an effort to curb Japanese aggression. The Japanese had taken control of Manchuria, Korea, Formosa and the Ryukyu and the Pescadores islands from China. Recognized since World War I as the world's third-ranking naval power, Japan felt it had outgrown its island kingdom and was bent on expansion. Japan continued to attack and conquer its neighbors throughout the 1930s, including a 1937 attack on Mainland China. After war broke out in Europe, a modernizing Japan sought to expand its influence, not only in Asia, but also throughout the entire Western Pacific. This doctrine resulted in escalating diplomatic tension with Washington.

After a Japanese attack on French Indochina (present-day Vietnam) in early 1940, Roosevelt took action against the Empire of the Rising Sun by imposing embargoes on scrap iron, steel and aviation fuel, followed by a freeze of Japanese assets in the United States. A further ban on all oil shipments was imposed by the British and Dutch.

On September 6, 1941, deep inside Tokyo's Imperial Palace, a fateful meeting was held. Present was Emperor Hirohito, the Son of Heaven, the 124th in an unbroken line of earthly deities reigning over the Japanese people for more than 2,600 years. While Hirohito reigned, however, he did not rule. That task belonged to the members of the Supreme Command and the Japanese cabinet. They discussed the desperate situation facing their nation. One by one, the foreign minister, the national planning board director and the navy chief of staff denounced the United States, Britain and the Netherlands as they described the economic sanctions that were strangling Japan. The Navy alone was consuming 400 tons of oil every hour. Unless the embargo was lifted, Japanese fuel reserves wouldn't last the year. It was decided that if Japan's diplomats could not negotiate away the sanctions by November, Japanese military forces would attack the territories of their enemies— including the American base at Pearl Harbor in Hawaii, the

British island fortress of Singapore and the Netherlands' East Indies. In the end, the diplomats failed, and the sanctions stayed in place.

Just before 8 AM on Sunday, December 7, 1941, the first wave of more than 200 planes, launched from Japanese carriers, attacked Pearl Harbor's Battleship Row. A second attack force of 170 planes swooped in an hour later. In less than 70 minutes, all the massive battleships of the U.S. Pacific Fleet were out of commission. Sunk and lost permanently were the *Arizona, Oklahoma* and *Utah*. Nearly 200 U.S. planes were destroyed, half of which never had time to get airborne. A total of 2,403 American soldiers and sailors were killed and another 1,178 injured. In stark contrast, the Japanese attackers—under the battle cry "Tora, Tora, Tora"—lost only 29 planes and fewer than 100 men.

Although every diplomatic development since October had pointed toward the likelihood of an attack on U.S. interests in the Pacific, the United States was caught totally off guard by the all-out Japanese aggression in Hawaii. American forces literally were caught sleeping despite reports as late as that very morning of ship and aircraft movements near the island of Oahu and the sinking of a Japanese "midget sub" at Pearl Harbor's entrance.

From Boston to San Diego, from Minneapolis to Miami, American outrage erupted over the Japanese attack. The venerable philosophy of isolationism died in the flames of the *Arizona* as she sank to the floor of Pearl Harbor. The following day—although 15 per cent of Americans opposed the action, according to the Roper Poll—America declared war on Japan. A few days later, Germany and Italy declared war on the United States.

The War to End All Wars had a sequel.

Long-range German artillery
(*Associated Press Photo*)

Doug Vink during a rare moment when
he was not in a Sherman tank

DOUG VINK

☆ ☆

He didn't realize it at the time, but growing up amid the brutal winters that are so much a part of life in Albany helped prepare Doug Vink for survival in what would be the most perilous challenge of his life.

Vink was born in January 1925, just beyond the northern edge of the city's downtown district. He drew his first breath on a street named for one of Albany's mayors, who tend to be serious local celebrities in a city where politics has been the primary industry for centuries. By American standards, Albany is an old town, founded by the Dutch more than three centuries ago. It consists of 225 miles of mostly narrow streets crammed into 21.5 square miles. Most of the year, it's a cold, dark place, with clouds blocking the sunlight four days out of 10. On an average day, the low temperature is 37 degrees and the high is 58, although the thermometer can soar and dive more than 100 degrees during the course of a year. Generally, the city endures freezing nighttime temperatures through the end of April, and the ice reforms in mid-October. In winter, frost digs its fingers into Albany soil an average of three feet down. One hundred inches of snow annually is not unheard of in New York state's capital city.

In 1925, the city was home to about 150,000 souls, including a New York City-born governor named Al Smith occupying the sprawling brick mansion on Eagle Street and a few hundred part-time state lawmakers who gleefully terrorized local taverns and bawdy houses for about half the year, when the Legislature was in session. The city huddled on the west bank of the Hudson River, 150 miles north of New York City, 225 miles south of Montreal, 175 miles west of Boston and 280 miles east of Buffalo. It was then and is now a hilly town. Albany's altitude ranges from 18 feet above sea level along the river's shore to 300 feet above sea level just west of the red-roofed state capitol building that overlooks the Hudson from the top of State Street Hill.

Vink grew up in a house on North Pearl Street, a few blocks west of the riverfront and near Albany's Palace Theater, a cavernous Vaudeville auditorium still in operation eight decades later. He was the second-youngest of 13 children. His father, Jacob Vink, was a native of Rotterdam, Holland. He'd come to America at age 18. Originally, Jacob Vink had settled to the west of Albany, in a tiny place called Dolgeville, where he had relatives. Later, he moved to Albany to find work as a yard conductor for the New York Central Railroad. Vink's mother, Mary, was an Albany girl whose family had its roots in County Cork, Ireland. Vink's was a particularly long-lived family. One of Doug Vink's great-grandmothers died at 101 years of age. The other reached 103.

Doug Vink came of age during the Great Depression. Jacob Vink earned about $35 a week on the railroad, and he had many mouths to feed. At age 13, Doug began helping out. He delivered groceries for a nearby meat market. He worked three hours every day after school and 12-hour days on Saturdays, bringing in about 10 bucks a week to help the family. The Vinks always ate well, but the younger kids wore hand-me-downs. They lived the way everybody they knew lived during those dark years. They never wanted, but there was never anything left over, either.

When World War II broke out, Doug Vink was a small-ish, wiry sophomore at St. Joseph's Academy on the corner of Second and Swan Streets. Pearl Harbor had so disturbed Vink's father that Jacob Vink refused to go to work for three days. A week after Jacob's son turned 18 in early 1943, he received a piece of mail from the Selective Service. He opened the envelope, read the document and informed his family, "This is it."

Doug Vink was the first of his family to be called. Later, his older brother, Henry, was drafted even though Henry was married and had four kids. Near the end of the war, the Selective Service System was grabbing whoever it could get. Henry Vink went into combat in Europe with just a few weeks training and came home with a bullet in his leg. Doug, already serving in Europe when Henry came over, never knew his older brother was there and never knew until after the war that Henry had been wounded.

Doug went for his draft physical at the Washington Avenue Armory, up the hill and about a dozen blocks to the west of his house. Army physicians proclaimed him sound and gave him seven days to wind up his personal affairs. He took the oath and entered the service on March 17th, only a few months before he'd been scheduled to graduate from high school.

On St. Patrick's Day 1943, Doug Vink reported for duty at the federal building on Broadway, several blocks southeast of the house in which he'd grown up. He was part of a party of 16 draftees. Both the day before and the day after, about 500 kids like him reported for duty and were shipped off to basic training. The U.S. Army captain supervising induction that day appointed Vink acting corporal of his group. The captain handed Vink a handful of chit cards and ordered him to lead his fellow inductees to a restaurant a few blocks away. Vink's job was to ensure that his comrades were fed decent breakfasts. He then was to lead them back to Broadway and into hulking Union Station, Albany's railroad passenger terminal near the federal building. There they were to board a train and begin their new lives as American soldiers. Pay was $75 a month. If they got into combat, they would receive a 10 per cent bump in salary for the period of time in which enemy soldiers had a chance to kill them.

The train took the group directly to Camp Upton in

Patchogue, N.Y., on the southern shore of eastern Long Island. There the group was assigned tents in which to sleep. In each tent, only a small, pot-bellied stove stood between the new soldiers and the March chill. They were issued uniforms and segregated into two groups based on their driving skills. Draftees who could operate automobiles were assigned to the infantry. Those who couldn't drive were assigned to the tank corps. Vink had never driven a car, sealing his fate as a tanker.

As a sergeant later explained to Vink's group, "Those guys know how to drive, and you can't teach them anything. When we get done, you'll all drive the same way."

After four days of processing at Camp Upton, the draftees were loaded onto trains and shipped off for basic training. For Vink, that meant transport to the Eighth Armored Division at Camp Polk. A day-and-a-half later, the train deposited him in a rural region of northern Louisiana. There the group was divided into platoons. Vink was issued his Army gear and a pack in which to carry it, which totaled 55 pounds fully loaded. The camp itself was divided into two sections—newer brick barracks in Polk's southern portion, aged wooden barracks in the north. Vink was assigned to a platoon housed in the older barracks.

For Doug Vink, basic training lasted 28 weeks—a period that was shortened later in the war. For the first eight weeks, the draftees were subjected to intense physical fitness regimens. They did calisthenics every morning. They routinely went on 25 and 50 mile hikes. Anywhere they went, they went at double-time, running constantly. In learning how to survive on foot on a battlefield, Vink was taught how to handle an M-1 rifle, a .30-cal. machine gun and a bazooka. With infantry training behind him, Vink then remained at Camp Polk for an additional seven months to be schooled in tank warfare. His first chore was learning how to drive the $95,000 Sherman tank—which operated not with a steering wheel but with steering handles, like a bulldozer—and to fire both its thundering 75 MM cannon and its murderous .50-cal. machine gun. He already knew how to handle its two .30-cal. machine guns, which were more accurate than the burlier .50-cal. atop the tank.

"The first time I got in a tank was scary," a white-haired Doug Vink said one day over breakfast in an Albany diner more than six decades later. "I'd never seen one before. . . . Eventually, I learned to drive the thing, though. Everybody did."

As assistant driver, Vink was also responsible for manning the tank's smaller machine gun, a .30-cal. weapon. Each member of a five-man tank crew had specific duties. The commander rode with his head outside the hatch, surveying the scene and directing both the driver and the guns. The gunner, charged with firing the tank's cannon, sat inside, in front of the commander, beside the loading end of his huge, booming weapon. The loader, the crew member whose job was to lift and insert the heavy, 18-inch shells into the tank's cannon in battle, also served as radio operator. Most cannon shells were stored beneath the tank's floor, prudently pointed downward. As assistant driver, however, Vink found himself sitting next to a second storage home for shells—a large rack of them. In all, the fighting machine carried about 100 shells into combat. Despite their assigned duties, each man in the crew was trained to perform every job in the tank.

Vink quickly grasped that the tank from which he was to fight was a rolling can of explosive, highly flammable material. Aside from its supply of shells, the gas tank was in the rear, less heavily armored than the front of the vehicle and vulnerable to a bomb from a plane, to a descending artillery shell or to a bazooka fired from behind. Vink was acutely aware that he was en route to a place where hundreds of thousands of German soldiers would be devotedly striving to blow up his tank, preferably with him inside it. That harsh reality was in his mind constantly at Camp Polk, as it was in the minds of all the green teenagers preparing to go to war against battle-tested troops 3,000 miles across the sea.

Sherman tanks carried 185 gallons of fuel, but they were voracious gas guzzlers. On the battlefield, they were heavily dependent on gasoline trucks—a convoy known as the Red Ball Express, the name emulated by hundreds of private trucking companies later started by vets across post-war America—to locate the machine at day's end and drop off five-gallon cans of fuel. It was because of the need for crew members to raise the armor plating to pour gas into the tank that the rear of the vehicle was relatively lightly armored.

Vink was trained in the use of the Colt .45-cal. automatic pistol, a tanker's only moderately accurate sidearm. It kicked ferociously but delivered slugs with terrific impact at close range. A tanker's rifle was the M-1 carbine, a shorter, lighter version of the basic M-1 infantry rifle. Tank crews, however, quickly found carbines impractical to carry inside the cramped confines of a Sherman tank. The only place in the vehicle to store the weapon was on the circular steel shelf on which the tank's turret rotated to deliver cannon fire. The carbines tended to get caught and sometimes crushed as the turret swirled, and they were famous for their inaccuracy. Ultimately, most of the carbines were discarded. Tankers came to prefer the "grease gun"—a short, fully automatic weapon with more firepower that took up less precious space inside the tank compartment. Throughout World War II, tankers scrambled out of the hatches of their fighting machines to grab grease guns whenever and wherever they came upon them on the battlefield. (In Europe later, Vink eventually came into possession of a 1928 Thompson submachine gun with a wooden stock, which he sawed off so he could store the weapon handily at his feet in the tank.)

Every Monday night, the troops marched five miles to what was known as "The Finger Bowl." That was a large outdoor arena with benches capable of holding the entire division. There the new troops would listen to what were supposed to be inspirational speeches by senior officers. The brass would tell the trainees what was expected of them. They warned the new soldiers against fouling up and threatened them with court martial if they did. Vink found none of this inspiring, instructive or amusing.

"You never had any entertainment," he said years later, "until Bob Hope showed up one time with Frances Langford. Now, that was a nice show."

In February 1944, the Eighth Armored Division went out on training maneuvers near Louisiana's Sabine River. Divided into a Red Army and a Blue Army, they played war games well into Texas, an exercise the troops ultimately found a waste of time. They understood that none of it counted unless somebody actually was shooting at you. Then orders arrived instructing all privates and privates-first class to return home before reporting back for duty not at Camp Polk but at Fort Meade, Md. From there, they would be shipped off to Europe as replacements for the 29,000 American soldiers killed and the 106,000 wounded in the D-Day invasion the previous June.

For Doug Vink and the other kids of the Eighth Armored Division, training was over. The time to fight was drawing near.

☆ ☆ ☆

After allowing for travel time, Doug Vink's 15-day furlough translated into just 10 days back in Albany. There he renewed acquaintances with old friends and looked around his home town for what he was acutely aware could be the last time. He told only his father that his next stop would be the European theater. Don't let your mother know, Jacob Vink urged. As requested, Doug told his mother nothing.

At Fort Meade, Vink and his buddies found all their equipment waiting for them. Again, they were housed in old wooden barracks. As they were processed for transport overseas, a month-long procedure, training continued. At 5:30 every morning, the men fell out in their shorts. They double-timed everywhere they went, often in full packs. They trekked off on long marches several times a week.

Other nights were their own and sometimes involved touring the bust-out bars in Baltimore, to which they journeyed by bus or on Army trucks, their trailers crammed with youthful soldiers who stood shoulder-to-shoulder for the entire trip. On weekend nights, Vink and the other partying soldiers slept in church steeples around Baltimore, courtesy of the churchs' womens guilds, which also supplied blankets and breakfast the next morning for hung-over servicemen.

Vink's best buddy during this period was a soldier from South Philadelphia whom he'd met at Camp Polk, Eddie Lamparski. At Meade, they served in different platoons but in the same company. They became constant leisure time companions, referred to by their comrades as "The Gold Dust Twins." Every day, Vink and Lamparski would visit the orderly room to see if their names were posted for departure. Then—seeing that they'd been spared for the day, and with training to be avoided if possible—they would try to find transportation to Baltimore. None of the newly inducted soldiers from around the nation felt the urge to travel a few more miles to Washington to tour the nation's capital.

"We figured they'd done enough dirt to us, taking us in," Vink recalled many years later. "But it was a big experience, and we were crazy enough to enjoy it, even though we didn't like the sergeants."

One morning, Vink saw his name on the board in the Fort Meade orderly room. He was to be transported to Camp Kilmer in New Jersey. At Kilmer, for several weeks the soldiers sat around the barracks while their personal clothing, especially any white civilian underwear, was confiscated. The Army wanted no combat soldier going overseas in possession of any item of clothing that could be used as a flag of surrender on the battlefield. Also confiscated was all American money, to be replaced in Europe with a special form of military currency known as "invasion money." At Kilmer, the daily routine was much the same as it had been at Fort Meade—hurry up and wait.

"Every day," Vink recalled later, "They'd tell you, 'Well, there's nothing for you to do today. You can go over to New York, if you want.' So, we'd jump on the bus and go over to

New York. Well, at that time we couldn't buy a drink because we were under age. You know, it was 21 at that time. So we went up to the old Interstate Bus Terminal, just around the corner from Grand Central Station. We'd walk in there. They had a bar. The owner said to us, 'How old are you?' We'd say, 'Eighteen.' He'd say, 'Well, if you're old enough to be in that uniform, you're old enough to drink.' So, we'd get our beer. But that was the only place. . . . Of course, he needed the business, too, probably."

Vink visited the orderly room daily for a few weeks until he finally saw his name on the board telling him to report back to the orderly room, with all his gear, at a specific time. Vink and the others were then loaded on a train and transported across the Hudson to disembark near Manhattan's Pier 90. As they stepped down from the train late on a hot day in May 1944, they gazed up at a gigantic Dutch ocean liner, the *New Amsterdam*, converted from luxury vessel to troop transport. They had no time to appraise the huge ship. Immediately, they were marched up the gangplank to the deck, high above the pier and the Hudson.

All vestiges of luxury had been stripped from the *New Amsterdam*. To accommodate 15,000 soldiers and 800 nurses en route to the European theater, the elegant ship had been relieved of every comfort. Now, there were no staterooms. Instead, men slept in tightly placed cots in every available space, including the empty swimming pool. The troops spent the night on the boat, getting used to these new accommodations, before the *New Amsterdam* pulled out in the morning. In its wisdom, the military had seen fit to provide the huge, crowded vessel with no naval escort. Four times, the captain was obliged to come about in the open sea and steam back at breakneck speed to the shelter of New York Harbor.

At first, Vink and the other men were baffled by the repeated retreats back through the Narrows. Crew members then explained why the *New Amsterdam* kept abandoning its journey and fleeing back into the harbor. In 1944, as American replacements were ferried across the ocean for the Allied push through France and into the Fatherland, German submarines were thick in the Atlantic waters just off the eastern United States.

"When we found out it was submarines," Vink recalled years later, "the rails were just lined with guys watching all the way over."

Eventually, the *New Amsterdam* was able to break free into the open waters of the North Atlantic. The vessel moved toward Europe via a northern route, passing Greenland and steaming steadily for the British Isles. As the ship zigged-zagged back and forth to thwart the submarine wolf packs, what should have been an eight-day trip stretched out to a dozen before the vessel put into port at Glasgow. From there, the troops were transported by train south into England to be deposited in a rural region near a farming town called Gurney Slade. There they took up residence in eight-man tents at a U.S. Army replacement depot—known throughout the Army as a "repple-depple."

Vink and his comrades had looked forward to seeing England, but their access to recreational facilities around the replacement depot was rationed carefully by the brass. The U.S. Army wanted no trouble with British locals, and a concentration of thousands of high-spirited young Americans preparing for entry into a war zone posed certain perils with regard to community relations. Vink and his buddies did frequent a pub owned by a family named Martin, who lavished hospitality on the young GI's.

"We got to know them pretty well," Vink recalled in later years. "They used to invite us up to their house for dinner on Sunday. But the first time we walked into that pub, you look, and there's the British Tommies over here, the Canadians are over here, the Australians are over here, and the New Zealanders are saying, 'Hey, Yank, come over here.' So, that's why the British hated us, the Tommies—because we sided in with the other guys. There's safety in numbers. . . . There was a lot of times that families would come up to you and invite you into the house, but the British guys didn't like us because we had all the girls."

Vink stayed in Gurney Slade for about five weeks, back in training every second he was on duty. Fifty-mile marches— 25 miles out, and 25 miles back in full pack after a half hour's rest—were the norm. Vink was 130 pounds of solid muscle, and none of his comrades carried any extra weight, either. The fact that the food was terrible helped in this regard. Vink never developed a taste for Spam and hominy grits, although he developed an unexpected affection for creamed, chipped beef on toast—referred to universally throughout the American military as "shit on a shingle."

One day in June, 10 days after the D-Day invasion, an officer entered the tent Vink called home in Gurney Slade and ordered him to gather his gear. A train transported Vink and 21 other men to Southampton, where they boarded somebody's private yacht—a sailing vessel of about 40 feet in length. The boat was operated by the U.S. Navy, one of hundreds used to ferry replacement troops across the English Channel to France. After D-Day, the military had sunk most of the larger vessels that had transported troops for the invasion to form a breakwater off Utah and Omaha Beaches in Normandy to facilitate the landing of replacements. As a result, those replacements were being moved across the Channel on any vessel that could be scrounged up. Crammed aboard the sailing yacht, and profoundly nervous about entering the open water in such a fragile craft, Vink and his 21 comrades crossed the Channel in fog.

After the sailing vessel crossed the breakwater of sunken ships and dropped anchor just off Omaha Beach, the replacement troops were ordered to jump into the chest-deep water in full packs and wade ashore.

"Of course, about 90 per cent of us couldn't swim," Vink recalled many years later. "I still can't. . . . Then they told us to sit on our packs. They came back in a while, that night, with trucks to pick us up. They took us up to St.-Lo to drop four of us off at the Sixth Armored Division, at Charlie Company."

Vink, his buddy, Eddie Lamparski, and two other men were introduced to the company commander, a Captain Hill, and then assigned to pitch two-man pup tents near a row of tanks. As Vink and Lamparski erected their new home, two French girls appeared. The girls had eggs they were eager to barter for gasoline. Vink and Lamparski convinced the girls to climb into the tent to inspect their quarters. The girls remained in the tent for a few hours. When the tent's flap finally was raised and the girls departed, Captain Hill called over to Lamparski and Vink.

"I can see you guys are going to make it in this outfit," the company commander said.

A few days later, the orders came. The Sixth was moving to Lorient, a German submarine base on the coast, to bombard subs as they came and went. Vink packed up his gear and moved to the tank to which he'd been assigned, number 75. It was a Sherman identical to the ones on which he'd received training in Louisiana, only this one was adorned on the side with the name "Sad Sack" in white lettering and a decal of a turtle in boxing gloves standing on its rear legs. It was a Walt Disney-designed symbol of the battalion nickname, "The Fighting Turtles." Beside the turtle was a large, white star, another of which adorned the top of the fighting machine.

With the other members of his crew, Vink climbed aboard in the order in which tanks crews had been trained to follow. The gunner entered first, then the loader, then the commander. The driver and assistant driver each entered through his own hatch. Vink was assigned to gunner duty. The tank's engine rumbled into life. The driver engaged his gears. The Sad Sack began to roll.

After 16 months of training and preparation, both physical and emotional, 19-year-old Doug Vink was finally going to war.

Omaha Beach, D-Day
(*Associated Press Photo*)

Tanks under production as the "U.S. War Machine"
is unleashed
(*Associated Press Photo*)

AMERICA GOES TO WAR

☆ ☆

Well before the attack on Pearl Harbor, the United States had begun unleashing its most powerful weapon on its enemies—the "U.S. War Machine." Pre-war industrial production under Roosevelt's lend-lease program had begun to pull America out of its decade-long economic crisis. By supplying the nearly bankrupt British and Soviet governments with much needed weapons, ships and munitions—based on a promise of future repayment—America was beginning to overcome the Great Depression.

The New Deal had eased the economic distress of the 1930s, but the war was ushering in an era of prosperity. From 1939 to 1945, the federal government increased its budget from $9 billion to $166 billion and paid for the increase by instituting the practice of requiring employers to withhold federal taxes from workers' paychecks. This was made palatable to Americans by forgiving them any 1941 taxes they might otherwise have owed the government on April 15, 1942.

The unemployment rate dropped from 15% in 1939 to 10% in 1941 to virtually full employment by 1943. With more than 12 million men soon to be bearing arms, women—most married and over the age of 35—were called on to enter the work force. From 1941 to 1943, five million "Rosie the Riveters" heeded the call to do their part to support the war effort.

The War Production Board oversaw the conversion of peacetime production to wartime production. The Office of

Price Administration ensured that shortages did not drive up the price of scarce goods. These were just two components of a newly created alphabet-soup of bureaucratic regulatory agencies whose function was to coordinate all phases of manufacturing and the economy. Shirt companies were converted to produce mosquito netting. Typewriter manufacturers fabricated machine guns. The auto industry turned out B-29 bombers.

Despite a new and unprecedented level of government regulation, corporate profits soared. Union membership increased to an all-time high, and "war boom" communities seemed to spring up overnight in what had been rural areas. Despite more government intrusion into their lives and shortages resulting in the rigid rationing of gasoline, meat and sugar—as well as the hardship of keeping old cars running, since no new vehicles were available after 1942—the American people planted their "victory gardens" and rose to meet wartime challenges without objection.

Ships were crucial to the war effort, both as a lend-lease commodity and as a means to transport supplies overseas. By 1941, British shipyards were unable to keep pace with the need to replace vessels falling victim to German submarines in the North Atlantic. Industrialist Henry J. Kaiser's solution was his creation of the "Liberty Ship." The process called for the fabrication of ships in sections at inland factories. These sections were then shipped and the vessels assembled at coastal shipyards. The first Liberty Ship was the *Patrick Henry*, launched in September 1941. Kaiser's plan called for a whirlwind assembly time of 80 hours and 30 minutes. By 1943, coastal shipyards were producing 140 seaworthy vessels a month, compared with only 102 built by conventional means in all of 1939.

Liberty Ships were only one example of the awesome rate at which American industry manufactured war goods. Most experts thought Roosevelt wildly optimistic when he set production targets of 100,000 planes and 50,000 tanks in 1941. The "War Machine" met and often exceeded his expectations. During World War II, American industry produced 300,000 aircraft, 88,000 landing craft, 215 submarines, 147 aircraft carriers, 952 warships, 86,333 tanks, 531 million tons of bombs and nearly 13 million rifles and carbines. By the end of 1944, American manufacturing capacity was more than double that of Germany and Japan combined.

With the U.S. Pacific Fleet devastated by the Pearl Harbor attack, the Japanese continued to press their advantage by attacking American bases in Guam and the Philippines. But on April 18, 1942, the U.S. military—although still not strong enough to battle in earnest—pulled off a daring air attack on Japan known as the "Doolittle Raid," named for Jimmy Doolittle, the officer who led the assault. The bombing of Tokyo and other Japanese cities sent a clear message to the startled enemy—the Japanese homeland was not safe. In May 1942, two American aircraft carriers, the *Lexington* and *Yorktown*—vessels safely out at sea during the Pearl Harbor attack—would make the enemy pay dearly for having overlooked them. The Battle of the Coral Sea would mark the first impediment to the Japanese advance. The Japanese strategy of landing at Port Moresby and cutting off Australia from the rest of the world failed to materialize. U.S. intelligence had intercepted and decoded enemy messages, allowing the Pacific Fleet's commander-in-chief, Admiral Chester Nimitz, to engage the Japanese and thwart their plans.

While the Battle of the Coral Sea would be considered a draw, with both participants losing aircraft carriers—the Lexington for the U.S. and the *Shoho* for the Japanese—the Japanese invasion was turned back, and the tide was turning in favor of the Allied forces. That would become even more evident on June 4, 1942, when the Harvard-educated Japanese admiral, Isoroku Yamamoto, would lead a strike on a strategic American Naval outpost on Midway Island. Yamamoto had been the mastermind of the attack on Pearl Harbor. He planned to finish the job by destroying the remainder of the Pacific Fleet. Once again, however, U.S. intelligence had intercepted his communications and learned of his plan, allowing Nimitz to ambush the unsuspecting Japanese as they initiated their assault on Midway. American bombers ultimately destroyed four aircraft carriers and effectively ended the Japanese offensive in the Pacific.

With the Pacific war beginning to turn in favor of the Allies, Roosevelt realized that Germany posed the larger threat to the free world. The meager 1.2 million-man army of Japan was stretched thin trying to maintain its Pacific conquests, including the vast territory of mainland China. Coupled with a lack of Japanese resources due to the economic embargos and the military losses they'd already sustained, the Empire of the Rising Sun was left with a doubtful capacity to launch any meaningful counterattacks.

With the invasion of the Soviet Union stalled by the brutal Russian winter, Hitler and his staff began working out plans for a "Final Solution" to what the Nazis regarded as "the Jewish Problem" in January 1942. This called for turning the Jews of Europe into a slave labor force that would be worked until they were dead or no longer needed. Those unable to perform heavy manual labor would be exterminated. Mass executions were carried out in Poland, at Auschwitz. Other concentration camps were being built at Sobibor, Treblinka, Belzec and Chelmno. More would come, all equipped with gas chambers capable of slaughtering thousands daily.

Russian Jews in occupied villages were given no chance to become part of the Nazi slave labor quotient. Their fate often consisted of digging their own graves—in the form of large, open trenches—before being machine-gunned. This duty was so horrific that even the brainwashed soldiers of the Third Reich were repelled, making it difficult for the Nazis to find enough troops to carry out the mass murders.

After the invasion of France and Russia, Britain stood essentially alone in the West against the Germans. Two thirds of the Allied military territory in Europe had either been captured or was under siege. Despite the widespread atrocities taking place, the United States was not yet ready to join the fight on European soil with a battle-tested adversary. In the spring of 1942, the Royal Air Force (RAF), under the new command of British Air Marshal Arthur Harris, changed its largely unsuccessful tactics of targeting primarily military sites and began attacking German cities with little regard for the safety of the civilian population. The war was now being taken to the German people. In July 1942, the United States joined the Brits and flew its first daylight raids against Germany.

It would not be until November 8, 1942, that American troops would fight on land. One hundred thousand troops, mostly Americans, landed in Morocco and Algeria. The Allies were not yet ready to fight the Germans in France, but the Soviet Union needed a second front opened up to divert Axis firepower. Operation Torch was led by General Dwight D. Eisenhower, who'd spent weeks in London urging the Combined Chiefs of Staff (the CCS, composed of the heads of British and American military services) to prepare for a 1943 invasion of France. In charge of all British and U.S. ground, sea and air forces, Eisenhower enjoyed a unique command in North Africa. He was the first army general ever to command wartime naval forces.

Before the landing, in June 1942, the British had suffered a humiliating defeat at the hands of the Axis army at Tobruk. Although outnumbered by the British, Hitler had sent his crack armored Afrika Corps under the command of General Erwin Rommel, known as the Desert Fox, to aid the Italians. The British garrison of 33,000 troops fell. Addressing the captured British officers at Tobruk, Rommel told them, "Gentlemen, you have fought like lions, but have been led by donkeys." After Tobruk, British forces were placed under the command of General Bernard Law Montgomery. Determined to take back their lost ground in Egypt, the British mustered an army of 195,000 troops and more than 1,000 tanks. Montgomery's faith in overwhelming numerical superiority in battle paid off in late October at El Amamein, where the German and Italian armies suffered 90,000 casualties. It was the first decisive Allied land victory of the war.

Bolstered by their success, the Brits continued to move west while Eisenhower's troops moved east in an effort to trap the Axis forces between the two armies in what was designed to be perhaps the greatest pincer movement in military history. Unfortunately, the green GI's were not up to defeating the battle-hardened German troops. Moreover, the superiority of German equipment became evident when American-made M-3 cannon shells merely bounced off German Panzer tanks. A lack of combat experience, ineffective weapons and massive air attacks by the Luftwaffe, the German air force, halted the American advance.

Montgomery, however, succeeded in chasing Rommel across North Africa in the direction of the American troops and into Tunisia. His problems with the British convinced Rommel that the Americans posed a less serious threat and could be dealt with successfully. Rommel believed that Americans were inferior to Germans as fighting men and looked forward to the opportunity to humiliate them in battle. He got his chance in February 1943. U.S. forces lost two battalions at Sidi Bou Zid as Rommel chased them across Tunisia. The battle at Kasserine Pass, however, would mark the final American defeat in North Africa.

In the end, Rommel's army was defeated by the effectiveness of British and American naval attacks on Italian and German supply ships. An Allied blockade of the ports of Tunisia effectively severed Axis supply lines. What the U.S. military lacked in experience was offset by a virtually endless stream of supplies and munitions. His own supplies dwindling, Rommel realized that the African campaign had failed. By the time the Afrika Corps surrendered to the Allies in May 1943, Rommel was back in Europe at Hitler's orders to deal with an anticipated Allied invasion of the continent somewhere along the French Coast.

While Americans were getting their first taste of combat and gaining confidence in their ability to confront what had been billed as a superior enemy, Roosevelt was lobbying for Allied forces to strike what could be a decisive blow against the Wehrmacht in France. However, British Prime Minister Winston Churchill felt the timing was not yet right to engage

Hitler on French soil.   In a compromise, Roosevelt and Churchill decided that once the Allies had secured victory in the North African campaign, they would invade Italy via the Mediterranean. The Germans, Churchill felt, were most vulnerable in what he described as the "soft underbelly" of Europe. The Allies, Churchill argued, could move into Italy, trap the Germans in an offensive staged through Greece and Turkey and effectively trap them between the British and Americans on one side and, on the other side, the Russians, who'd begun to turn the tide on the Eastern Front and were rapidly regaining lost territory.

After the German surrender in North Africa, the Allied landing in Sicily was dubbed Operation Husky and scheduled for July. Assigned to lead the campaign was Lt. General George S. Patton, nicknamed "Old Blood and Guts," a veteran tank commander noted for his highly polished boots, pearl-handled revolvers and a blunt-spoken aggressiveness seldom found in politician-soldiers with stars on their shoulders. Patton was to prepare the U.S. Seventh Army, working in concert with the British Eighth Army, for an assault on Sicily. Patton met only pallid resistance from the Italian defenders. The Germans, however, continued to fight hard and managed to keep open an escape route across the Straits of Messina and onto the Italian peninsula. In August, after 38 days of combat, most of the German troops fled from Sicily.

During the Allied assault on Sicily, the Italian dictator, Benito Mussolini, was arrested and his fascist government overthrown. Later, his power partially restored by Hitler's troops, Mussolini was captured and lynched by Communist partisons. A few weeks after Sicily fell, a new Italian government declared it was joining the Allies. Incensed, Hitler poured fresh troops into Italy and demanded that Field Marshal Albert Kesselring stand fast against the Allied advance.

On September 9th, U.S. and British troops landed on the Italian mainland at Salerno, just south of Naples. What began as a relatively non-eventful landing turned bloody when

German counterattacks nearly split the beachhead in half. Massive air and naval artillery attacks finally allowed the Allies to gain control the southern third of the Peninsula below Naples by early October.

Despite Churchill's optimistic predictions, Italy would prove to be anything but a "soft underbelly." Hitler's forces mounted a fierce defense. Aided by what generals refer to as "good ground"—natural obstacles like high mountains, swift rivers and rocky spurs—the Wehrmacht kept control of hilltops and ridges along the narrow coastal plains, allowing them to rain down artillery fire on Allied troops and vehicles as they attempted to push forward. The German defensive formation, known as the Gustav Line, stretched 120 miles across Italy. Both sides remained locked in battle in the mud and cold throughout the winter of 1943-1944. Any attempt to advance by the combined armies of the United States, Britain, Poland, Morocco, New Zealand and Canada resulted in heavy Allied casualties. The fighting was as brutal as any seen since the trench warfare of the First World War.

After failing to make headway, the Allies staged a landing behind German lines at Anzio on January 22, 1944. The beachhead was only 30 miles from the prize of Italy, the city of Rome. Hitler ordered Kesselring to crush the invasion. New German troops and weapons poured into the beachhead, pinning down the Allies for more than four months.

As fighting raged at Anzio, the Allies attempted another offensive aimed at a German stronghold on the western Italian coast near the 1,400 year-old Benedictine monastery at Cassino. After three bloody assaults that resulted in the old fortress being bombed into rubble, the Allies were still unable to break through the Gustav Line.

It would not be until mid-May—after a savage, bloody battle—that Polish Allied troops finally would gain control of the hilltop at Monte Cassino. Air attacks on railways and bridges would disrupt the Axis supply line. Fresh Allied soldiers trained in mountain warfare would replace veterans, who were sent back to England to prepare for a major offensive elsewhere.

After breaking out of the Cassino region in May, Allied tanks finally were rolling toward Rome. Patton had been recalled to England as a result of several controversial incidents—including slapping battle-fatigued soldiers in a field hospital and delivering a speech to his troops that seemed to encourage savage treatment of the enemy. His replacement, General Mark Clark, made a serious error. Instead of moving his troops east and cutting off the enemy retreat, which could have ended the Italian campaign much earlier, he chose instead to become the high-profile liberator of Rome. This mistake would allow Kesselring and his troops to slip away. Clark's decision resulted in more than another year of fighting before the Allies could liberate Italy. As the war ended in May 1945, the Germans still held the Italian Alps.

What began as a promising plan to attack Hitler through his back door had degenerated into a quagmire of lost lives and opportunity. The Italian campaign had delayed a buildup for what what had, from the start, been the heart of the Allied strategic plan to defeat the Third Reich.

The invasion of France.

Al Cohen

Standing behind the table with the Nazi flag, Al Cohen holds the mike in his right hand, clutching the cord in his left. He's a subdued, soft-spoken man with a manner that radiates gentleness. He gazes up at the rows of students rising above the spot at the bottom on the amphitheater where the veterans have set up for their presentation.

"The weather was cold," he says. "It was below zero. Think back about two weeks ago, with all of that deep snow that we had. Think about if you had to sleep in that, live in that, day in and day out, without having a warm place where you could get out of the wind. That's what we went through. We didn't have enough winter clothing. We had these [uniform] pants, matching . . . shirt, long underwear, a sweater, and we had overcoats. The problem with the overcoats was that when they got wet, instead of weighing about twenty pounds, they weighed about sixty pounds. So, everybody got rid of those, and we just used the field jacket. They had no liners in them—and it was cold.

"We very seldom got any hot food. Everything was in canned rations—K-rations or C-rations. Usually, they were frozen. You had no way of lighting a fire. You lit a fire, and the Germans would see it."

He picks up a World War II infantry helmet that rests atop the table and displays it for the students.

"You couldn't wash," Al Cohen tells them. "If you were able to put some snow in a helmet—if you were in one place long enough to put snow in the top part of your helmet, and if you could melt it— you could wash and brush your teeth. The water in your canteen would freeze. You had nothing to drink unless you ate snow—if it was clean. If it wasn't clean, then you ended up with diarrhea. . . ."

AL COHEN

☆ ☆

On the sunny Sunday morning that Japanese war planes attacked Pearl Harbor, Al Cohen was a somewhat shy, slim high school kid living 6,000 miles away from the carnage. Immediately, he made up his mind to enlist. No, his mother told him; you're not going. I have to go, he said. Not now, she said to him; wait. So, festering, 16-year-old Al Cohen waited.

Lillian Cohen's reluctance was understandable. Al was her only child, and she hadn't seen his father in eight years. Joe Cohen had operated a tire business in Oswego, N.Y. When that hadn't worked out, Joe had gone to New York City, establishing his wife and young son in an apartment at 95th Street and Riverside Drive on Manhattan's upper west side. He'd gone to work in a cafeteria operated by a cousin in a New York City office building. Then the cousin gave up the business. Joe Cohen started selling shoes and, apparently, hated it. One night, he told his wife he was going out. He never came back.

Lillian Cohen had been Lillian Strosberg, the daughter of an Albany tailor. She took her little boy and moved back to the New York state capital, where she'd met Joe Cohen at a yacht club dance years before. She moved in with a sister. Later, Lillian got a good job managing a dress shop and found her own place a few blocks south of the New York governor's mansion, right across the street from a nice public park. Al Cohen grew up in that apartment, with his grandmother and an uncle as members of the household.

He attended Philip Schuyler High School, named after a Revolutionary War general who became a U.S. senator. At 16, Al Cohen quit school to join the military, but his mother refused to sign for him. Instead, Cohen then went to work at a U.S. Army Corps of Engineers depot at the Port of Albany on the west bank of the Hudson River. He and a friend, Irwin Feldman, began visiting every recruiting office they could locate, lying about their ages and trying desperately to enlist.

"They would look at the two of us," Cohen recalled decades later, "and he was a big, husky guy, and I was a skinny kid, and the recruiter would look at him and think, 'There's the kind of guy we want.' And they'd look at me and go, 'Eh?' But he had a punctured ear drum. They wouldn't take him. So, finally, we took the train one day, and we went down to New York to the maritime service. We tried to join the Merchant Marine. . . . I still have the letter they sent me to report for training, but my mother wouldn't sign."

Desperate to serve, but unable to enter any branch of the regular military without Lillian Cohen's signature, Al Cohen joined the New York Guard, a state-sponsored reserve force. He attended weekly drills, learning to use weapons, learning military routines and procedures. He wasn't really in the war, though, and the New York Guard wasn't the sort of service for which he lusted. At age 17, Al Cohen and Irwin Feldman managed to get friendly with a U.S. Coast Guard recruiter who liked to hang around Albany's Jewish Community Center. We want to join, they told him. The recruiter arranged for physicals for both boys. Feldman, with his punctured ear drum, was rejected. Cohen passed a cursory physical by a civilian doctor and finally convinced his weary mother to sign his Coast Guard enlistment papers. Then it was off for Manhattan Beach in Brooklyn for processing and training. Finally, Al Cohen was in the service, even if it was a service that wasn't seeing much combat action. His Coast Guard career, however, didn't last long.

A military doctor had seen something he didn't like. Al Cohen had some sort of spot on his lung that, in the view of the

Coast Guard, rendered him unfit for service. A Coast Guard physician told him he was out—that he should go home, get a nice easy job, avoid exerting himself and try to live a long life. Cohen went back to Albany and got a job on a riveting gang in a locomotive factory. His mother was panicked about his health, so he went to a prominent Albany physician, underwent still another physical examination and found himself pronounced completely sound.

Now Lillian Cohen really had something to worry about. Al was determined to get into the Army. When he turned 18 in October of 1943, he immediately registered for the draft. On the form, he was asked if he had previous military service. Al Cohen made a point of leaving that section blank. He wasn't about to alert the draft board to his ejection from the U.S. Coast Guard. Not long after, as he'd expected, Al Cohen was called for his draft physical. He was handed a folder and moved in his underwear from station to station, from doctor to doctor. The final physician opened the folder. Inside it, scrawled in pencil, was Cohen's dismissal from the Coast Guard for reasons of ill health.

"This last doctor sees it," Cohen recalled. "He says, 'Did you want to get out?' I said, 'No, I would have given anything to serve—work in the office, clean pots and pans, anything they wanted to stay in.' So, he says, 'Your physical here was okay. We'll call you back again in three months for another physical.' So, three months go by. I go back for another physical. This time I took an eraser with me. . . . So, they hand you the papers, and right away I knew what section the problem would be in. So, I looked through it. The section was now blank. I didn't say a word. I went through the physical. And that was it; I went in. . . . Somebody forgot to type it in on the new papers."

Al Cohen quit his job at the locomotive works and spent the next 10 days partying with friends, celebrating the successful conclusion of his more than two-year struggle to get into World War II. Then he and perhaps a dozen other young guys were shipped off by train from Albany to Fort Dix, N.J.

There they were issued uniforms, given vaccinations against various ailments, had their hair shaved off, took some aptitude tests and were loaded aboard another train. They arrived three days later at Camp Joseph T. Robinson, an infantry training facility just outside Little Rock, Ark. Camp Robinson was a collection of pressed board huts on cinder block pilings, each with a pot-bellied stove in the middle of the barracks—an utterly vestigial piece of equipment in the 100-plus degree temperatures of August in Arkansas.

Infantry basic lasted 17 weeks. It began with calisthenics and moved on to heavier physical conditioning. Initially, the trainees simply marched around the camp, startled to discover that German prisoners of war were on the premises. Then came weapons training, and lots of it—with the M1 rifle, with machine guns and bazookas and Browning Automatic Rifles, with the .45-cal. Colt automatic pistol. The troops underwent demolition training, learning how to set explosive charges. They crawled on their bellies through what was called the infiltration course, with live machine gun slugs whizzing just over their backs. The new recruits ran everywhere, usually weighed down by rifles and field packs. Because Cohen had the benefit of some military training in the New York Guard, he found himself designated an acting corporal.

A few times a week, the trainees ran a bayonet course, moving through a stand of woods with cardboard dummies of German soldiers popping up in front of them to be bayoneted. At the end of the bayonet course lay a large grassy field used for parade practice. One morning the trainees came running out of the woods into the field to find the German POW's policing it—picking up paper and other debris under the watchful eyes of MP's with shotguns. As playful, shouting young soldiers with bayonets charged in their direction, the POW's scattered with the MP's shouting and chasing after them.

"After the third time that happened," Cohen recalled, "they changed their policing schedule."

One morning the training sergeants took Cohen and his

buddies out into a field where loads of telephone poles had been deposited. The troops divided into teams and, under the direction of the training sergeants, began tossing the telephone poles at one another. After months of that intense conditioning regimen, Cohen felt better physically than he'd ever felt before. Training ended with two weeks living in pup tents in the field, capped off with a 30-mile hike in full, 60-pound field packs.

"If you didn't make it," Cohen recalled, "if you had to fall out, you had to start the whole training cycle over again."

During the 17 weeks, the troops spent most nights in blackface learning how to wage war in darkness. During that period, they got into Little Rock perhaps three times—breaks in the training routine that they used mainly to escape Army food and eat in restaurants with white tablecloths. Little Rock crawled with GI's, but they were not warmly received by the locals. The first Army unit at Robinson had gleefully impregnated a disturbing number of local girls, earning the Army a lasting enmity from the permanent residents of Little Rock.

On Christmas Eve 1944, a sergeant entered the barracks to inform Cohen and several others that they had a half hour to get packed. They were going home. Cohen spent four days back in Albany before reporting to Fort Meade, Md., for more shots and a clothing check. During the few days he underwent processing at Meade, Cohen had no time to get into Baltimore, where his father was living at the time. He was then loaded on a train and shipped off to Camp Kilmer, N.J. At Kilmer, he and the other men in his detachment were marched through a warehouse and issued new M1s and bayonets. In the barracks, they cleaned the packing grease from the rifles. They ate and, as darkness fell, were transported to a ferry on the western shore of the Hudson River. The ferry took them to a pier at 32nd Street in Manhattan. Looming up next to the pier in the light cast by Manhattan skyscrapers was a huge ship—the *Queen Elizabeth*, Cohen later learned.

Cohen later recalled, "Some of the guys were yelling, 'We live only a few blocks from here.' We were kibitzing and all, and we got up to the pier, and we were all lined up, and everybody was joking. The Red Cross was there, giving us coffee and doughnuts. Then, over the loudspeaker, we heard, 'When your last name is called, sound off with your first name and middle initial.' And all of a sudden you could hear a pin drop. Nobody was joking any more."

In the silence of that frigid January night on Manhattan's west side, the reality of the situation now fully upon them, the troops were marched up the gangplank to the deck of the *Queen Elizabeth*. The once luxurious ocean liner was now no more than a gigantic floating barracks designed to move as many as 27,000 men to Europe on every voyage. Cohen found himself assigned to a canvas cot in a stateroom he was to share with 15 other men who were stacked three high along the bulkhead. He knew that these were relatively posh accommodations. In the hold, located in the bowels of the huge vessel, Cohen's comrades were sleeping in vertical rows 12 high, scrambling up ladders to crawl into bed.

Just before dawn, the *Queen Elizabeth* pulled away from the pier. Tugs guided her into New York Harbor as the sun rose over the city's towering spires. Cohen and others made their way to the starboard rail to study the Statue of Liberty as the massive ship glided by the island from which Lady Liberty presided over New York's watery doorway.

"It was an odd feeling," he recalled many years later. "It's not fun and games any more. That's when it sinks in on you—you're going."

Once through the Narrows and into the open sea, the *Queen Elizabeth* steamed south along the New Jersey coast to steer clear of what might be left of the German submarines coming in from the North Atlantic to prowl outside the path to New York Harbor and hunt American troop transports. Finally, the great vessel turned left and moved northeast. Four days later, the ship dropped anchor at a little town on the coast of Scotland.

"It was dawn," Cohen said. "You could see the fields of heather, the white thatched-roof cottages. And you could see all these torpedo boats running around. They took us off on lighter, smaller boats. We got on the dock. They lined us up, and there were some railroad cars there. They loaded us on. They told us to keep the shades down."

The train took Cohen and the other troops to Plymouth, on Britain's eastern shore. It was a Friday night. One of the sergeants told Cohen that if he were not called that evening to board a boat bound for France, he would get a weekend pass to London. It was a prospect that intrigued him, but as the thousands of troops milled about the Plymouth docks they learned that they were being chosen for boarding by name, in alphabetical order. Instead of prowling Trafalger Square in search of British women, Al Cohen found himself loaded aboard a large commercial vessel with no bunks. He slept on the deck as the ship crossed the 20-mile-wide English Channel.

In the morning, the thousands of green troops were taken off the vessel on landing craft and landed at Le Harve, a seaport town at the mouth of the Seine. They were marched through what was left of the bombed-out city as a swarm of French children buzzed around them begging for candy and cigarettes. Atop a hill outside the city, the troops were left off at a sprawling, muddy encampment of 16-man tents to sleep on the ground in the January chill. The following morning, the GI's were loaded on boxcars in groups of about 60 and transported inland to Metz, a journey of about a day. The men slept as the boxcars rumbled and clanked on the tracks until they were dropped off at a replacement depot. They were then marched across the snowy countryside to another camp, to what had once been a French cavalry post. A huge stone barn dominated the place, flanked by old masonry barracks. Cohen's first sensation upon arrival was the severity of the cold.

"We got up to this room where we were assigned," he recalled, "a whole bunch of us, and there was straw on the floor, and no heat. They fed us there that day. The next day they took us out to a rifle range in a field. They had straw bales set up as targets. We were supposed to sight in our rifles, but I couldn't do it. It was so damn cold that my fingers couldn't operate the rifle's adjustments. They gave you a clip of ammunition to sight it in. I just fired it off."

That night, Cohen and others were loaded aboard four two-and-a-half-ton trucks. The canvas covers designed to shelter the vehicles' beds were rolled back to permit the men quick and easy escape in the event of an air attack. The trucks rolled through the frigid darkness for perhaps three hours, the replacement troops huddled and shivering in the rear of each vehicle. Finally, the truck in which Cohen was riding entered Luxembourg City and immediately broke down. Cohen and his buddies sat freezing in the dead truck until a Jeep containing four MP's rolled up behind the truck and stopped. In the ensuing conversation, the MP's learned that these men were fresh replacements who hadn't yet had the chance to exchange their greenbacks for invasion money. Hospitably, the MP's then pulled out rolls of invasion money and spread it around, refusing to take any American currency in exchange. Immediately, the freezing troops abandoned the truck and headed for a tavern. They shot down cup after cup of coffee laced with liquor, but their hands remained so cold and stiff that none of them could even manage to button the flies of their uniform pants after using the restroom.

Eventually, another truck rolled up outside the tavern. The troops were called outside to pile aboard. After using the rest of the MP's invasion money to load up on bottles of wine, they did just that. The new truck continued its journey with the replacements in the open bed in back sharing bottles of wine to keep their blood flowing in the bitter cold. North of Luxemburg city, the driver slammed on the brakes. A squad of MP's had blocked the road.

Cohen recalled, "I heard them say, 'Where the hell are you going?' So the driver says, 'I got replacements for the 90th.' The MP says, 'Another 10 feet and you'll give them to the Germans.' This was Bastogne. The driver had missed a turn and overshot. He really got that truck turned around fast."

Cohen and his buddies were ferried past the wreckage of war—burned out tanks and piles of debris that had once been some sort of military vehicle. Ultimately, they were dropped off at the headquarters of the 90th Infantry Division. They spent the rest of that night trying to sleep in bed rolls in a bombed-out church next to a cemetery that also had been bombed. Caskets had been blasted from the dirt and lay about in profusion. The following morning, they were marched to the front lines about five miles from Bastogne. At battalion headquarters, the group was solicited for volunteers for heavy weapons duty.

"This one group of us," Cohen recalled, "we came over on the ship together, and we'd been through the replacement depot together. And here we were, still together. So, when they wanted volunteers for heavy weapons, some of the guys said, 'Let's volunteer for the mortar platoon. We'll be in the back of the lines.' Some of us figured, 'What the heck. We know each other. This way we'll stick together.' So, we volunteered, too. . . . We got assigned to our company, M Company, and we find out that we're machine gunners, not mortar men."

Once the group arrived at their platoon headquarters, they found out why the brass had been so eager for machine gunners. After D-Day and the early days of the Battle of the Bulge, only three men remained of the original 60 in the platoon. That night, Cohen's group was given training on the .30-cal. water-cooled machine gun. The following morning, while loading a machine gun aboard a Jeep, one of the veterans was wounded in the hip by a round left in the weapon's chamber and shipped off to a hospital. Another veteran suffered from frozen feet. He was transferred to a tank unit to spare him from walking into combat. That left only one experienced man to work with about a dozen green replacements. They worked in three-man crews per gun.

It was only a few days later that the heavy weapons unit came under fire from small arms and artillery. They saw no one, but they heard the reports of the weapons directed at them. Everyone was frightened, but no one was hit. When the firing ended, all the men felt a terrific sense of exhilaration at having escaped death or injury. After that, the sound of enemy weaponry always focused their attention, but they'd learned an oddly comforting truth about warfare. Years later, Al Cohen summed it up.

"The one that gets you," he said, "that's the one you never hear."

Source: *United Press International*

THE INVASION

☆ ☆

"Unity, coordination and cooperation are the keys"
—General Dwight D. Eisenhower

General Dwight David Eisenhower was one of seven sons born into a poor Texas family. His devoutly Christian parents, David and Ida, had raised him and his brothers on a paycheck that had never exceeded $100 a month. A West Point graduate who'd impressed his superiors with his judgment and political skills, Eisenhower was selected by President Roosevelt as Supreme Commander of the Allied military forces. Eisenhower was to prepare and lead a multinational force in the invasion of France. Roosevelt believed in Eisenhower's ability to deal with expansive egos and forge cooperation among Allied leaders. The operation was predominantly American in design and bravado. The British had argued for a more cautious, limited approach. Roosevelt and America wanted to meet the enemy head on.

Eisenhower was delighted when, in December 1943, he'd been recalled to London, and relieved of command of the slow, arduous, Italian campaign. Instead, he was to prepare and take charge of the largest single undertaking ever attempted by man—the Allied invasion of Europe. He was well aware of the incalculable risk of such an event and that the entire course of the war hinged on the success or failure of what had been dubbed Operation Overlord. He would be assisted by a staff of over 16,000 officers and enlisted men and bolstered in the field by his chief U.S. commanders. Among them were General Omar Bradley, a fellow West Point graduate and Eisenhower's close friend, and General George Patton, whom Eisenhower had backed when others were calling for his dismissal after several unpopular incidents in Italy. Field Marshal Bernard Law Montgomery would command British forces. While Ike, as Eisenhower was known, respected Montgomery's ability, they were often at odds over military strategy.

The plan called for 156,000 men from three nations to hit the French beaches at five locations. More than 6,000 ships and thousands of planes of every variety would back them. Before the attack, Eisenhower demanded that bombing raids be switched from Germany to France to cut German lines of communication. He was determined to deny the enemy a swift reply to the invasion with reinforcements once the Allies had landed. When Ike met with resistance from Allied air commanders, he threatened to resign if the bombers were not reassigned. In January 1944, the bombing raids began. After consulting weather and tide charts, Eisenhower decided on an invasion through Normandy, located in Northwestern France along the English Channel, between the regions of Picardy and Brittany. The invasion was scheduled for June 5, 1944.

The Germans knew an attack was on the horizon, but they didn't know when or where it would take place. General Erwin Rommel, who had plagued the Allies in North Africa, was in charge of defending the French coastline. He controlled two armies—one at Calais and one stationed further southwest in Normandy and Brittany. He expected the Allies to come ashore across the narrowest part of the English Channel at Calais. That expectation was fed by a huge, fictitious military buildup staged under Patton. Code-named Fortitude, the elaborate ruse included construction of bogus barracks and depots. The Allies used Ultra, a complex intelligence operation that employed a smuggled version of a German code machine called Enigma, to break what Hitler had thought to be an unbreakable code. Through Ultra, the Allies knew that the Germans were swallowing the bait.

The actual amphibious invasion taking place south of where the Germans had concluded the Americans would land called for Allied forces to come ashore at five beaches. Those beaches were code-named Utah and Omaha, where Americans would land; Juno, the site of the Canadian landing, and Sword and Gold, where British troops would come ashore. Three airborne divisions would use parachutes and gliders to infiltrate further inland to protect the flanks of the invading forces. The U.S. Navy would hover off shore and use big guns to soften enemy defenses before landing. Allied planes would patrol to ward off any counterattacks by the Luftwaffe, which had been badly weakened during the air raids of the previous five months.

Rommel understood the need to meet and defeat the Allies on the coast. He knew that once they obtained a foothold on the continent that they would be enormously difficult to remove. The Desert Fox and his chief confidante, Vice Admiral Friedrich Ruge, often discussed the upcoming invasion and the overwhelming air superiority the allies would enjoy. Forty days before the attack, Admiral Ruge wrote in his diary that the disparity between the Luftwaffe and the Allied air forces was "humiliating".

As what the Allies called D-Day neared, Eisenhower worried about weather conditions. Heavy squalls had created five-foot waves on the beaches, making it all but impossible for tanks and troops to land successfully. If he delayed, Ike knew, then plans that had been two years in the making might have to be scrapped. With more than 160,000 troops in on the plan, news of Allied intentions was bound to leak to the enemy sooner or later. On the other hand, landing during a storm could turn the invasion into a mass suicide. After much angst on the part of the Supreme Commander and a tense debate with his subordinates—which resulted in a 24-hour delay of the mission because of the hazardous weather conditions—the invasion was launched on June 5, 1944. Within hours, an armada of more than 6,000 vessels departed docks in southern England. The largest movement of men and machines in history was underway.

As trucks were loaded on supply ships leaving from Dover, the line grew so long that a gridlock formed, and an ice cream truck stuck in the middle of the mess was sent to France along with Allied forces. The war's biggest gamble was now in motion. A fretful Eisenhower reportedly prepared a statement in case the operation ended in failure.

While the ships carrying American, British and Canadian troops rocked as the sea churned from the heavy squalls, 822 aircraft carrying 23,400 paratroopers—and many planes hauling gliders—roared over the heads of seasick infantrymen. The paratroopers and gliders were to be dropped deeper into the Normandy countryside well behind the beach. Eisenhower, knowing how critical and extremely dangerous this night drop behind enemy lines was, walked among his soldiers, asking where they were from and slapping shoulders prior to the invasion force's departure from Portland Bill on the English coast. He stayed until the last plane, carrying the 101st and 82nd Airborne Divisions, had left on its mission, well aware that many paratroopers would not be returning.

Heavy fog and German ground fire interfered with pilots and kept them from dropping the men in precise position in the drop zone at the base of the Cotentin Peninsula. The 101st suffered heavy casualties. Only one-sixth of the men made it to their pre-planned destination points. Some were dropped so far off target that they landed in the sea and drowned under the weight of the 100-plus pounds of equipment they carried. Others were hit by anti-aircraft fire before they could exit the planes or were dropped too low to give their chutes time to open.

The most dangerous mode of transport into Normandy proved to be the glider. Whole crews were killed in these "flying coffins" when they smashed into hedgerows or "Rommel's asparagus"—poles erected in open spaces by the Germans to inhibit glider landings.

The 82nd Division's first regiment fared better than the 101st, but the Second Regiment was unable to retrieve its supplies, leaving many of the men insufficiently armed. Most were dropped much farther apart than planned and had to scurry around to find each other without alerting the enemy. Using hand clickers that sounded like crickets to locate comrades and mass together, the troops formed makeshift groups and went about carrying out their mission. In spite of huge casualties, the 101st and 82nd, working in concert with the British Sixth Airborne Division, engaged the enemy and succeeded in capturing bridges, crossroads and other strategic positions, helping to ensure that the beach landings would be safe from a German counterattack.

On June 6th, around 6:30 AM, the first seaborne units began arriving along the 50 miles of Normandy coastline. They were ushered in by the thunder of large Navy guns pounding the German defenses. The British and Canadians at Sword, Gold and Juno beaches, as well as the Americans landing at Utah Beach, met with only light resistance. This was due in part to the surprise of the landing sites and the fact that the Germans had not expected an invasion immediately after such harsh weather. Rommel was so certain that no invasion would be staged that he reportedly was back in Germany celebrating his wife's birthday. His absence severely hampered enemy response time to the attack.

Americans landing at Omaha Beach, the code name for the second beach from the right of the five landing points, suffered the misfortune of arriving during a training exercise of Germany's veteran 352nd Infantry Division and met extreme resistance. The largest of the assault zones, Omaha Beach measured more than six miles wide, with a third of the terrain protected by a 10-foot-high seawall and the entire area surrounded by cliffs. The enclosed battlefield had only five exits. The best was a paved road leading to the village of Vierville-sur-Mer. Two were dirt roads and two were only dirt paths.

Rommel had built formidable defenses to protect the area—including beach and water mines, resistance nets and countless fighting posts accessed via an elaborate trench system.

Omaha Beach became a killing zone as the Americans were attacked from fixed weapons that covered the beach as well as firepower raining down from the cliffs above. The landing also was hindered by high seas that filled the landing craft, drowning many of the troops inside. Sherman tanks outfitted with special floatation screens designed to enable them to "swim" ashore were toppled by the surf and sank. Oil fires from slicks on the water created a sea of fire as soldiers desperately fought to get ashore.

Seventy-five percent of men in the first wave were killed before reaching shore. Some, screaming in terror, tried to get back to the boats, but there was nowhere to run. Reaching shore and then getting off the beach was their only slim chance of survival as German gunners zeroed in on them. Those able to make it off the boats sought cover behind various beach obstacles as they sprinted over the open stretch to the relative safety of the seawall at the cliff's base.

Bradley, leading the U.S. First Army, at one point considered calling off the landings in favor of attempting to come ashore at a different point. Little by little, however, the Americans clawed their way off the beach and, working in small groups, managed to scale the cliffs. Navy destroyers moved into point blank range, so close that they were scraping bottom in the shallow water, and began bombarding German Defenses. By 1200 hours, enemy fire began to fade. The Omaha Beach exits began opening up. By nightfall, the areas around Omaha and the other landing sites were secure. The Americans were holding positions around Vierville, Saint Laurent and Colleville, short of where they'd hoped to end up, but they'd achieved their toehold in Hitler's "Fortress Europe." American casualties exceeded 2,400, but by the end of the day they'd inflicted 1,200 casualties on the German 352nd, depleting almost 20 per cent of its strength. And, unlike the Allies, the Germans had no replacements en route to continue the fight.

Hitler had left strict orders not to be disturbed. Consequently, the Fuhrer slept through the invasion. He'd promised to give the Allies the thrashing of their lives if they invaded France. While the Germans dealt death promiscuously at Omaha beach, they'd failed to halt the invasion. Now, with Allied air forces securing the hard-won landing territory, the invading troops were off the sand and on their way into the Normandy interior. By the end of June, the Allies had established positions 20 miles inland. Almost a million men, a half million tons of supplies and more than 175,000 vehicles had been transported to France for the push east toward Paris and then the Rhine.

The German High Command had taken a full day to realize that the Normandy invasion was not a distraction to cover the real assault at Calais further north. Had Hitler not insisted on sleeping, he may have exhibited the savvy to send his crack tank corps to the front instead of holding them in reserve for the "real" attack they expected from Patton's fake army. By the time Third Reich commanders realized that the Normandy invasion was genuine, they'd lost their chance to mount an effective counterattack. Allied paratroopers operating behind the German lines added to the defenders' chaos.

After leaving the beaches, the Americans were to cut off the Cotentin Peninsula to the west while the British Second Army moved to capture the city of Caen. The Allies still needed to capture ports to continue their buildup of men and supplies. While the beaches at Normandy had been secured, the region lacked a natural harbor from which to offload essentials. Two Mulberries, or artificial harbors, that the Allies had built had fallen victim to a storm that struck a few days after D-Day.

Securing inland objectives was a bloody business. Fighting moved off the beaches to the "hedgerows" of the Normandy countryside—dense strips of vegetation that provided excellent cover for the counterattacking Germans and the invading Allied soldiers to advance along narrow paths between the thick foliage. Allied air support was rendered ineffective by the close-quarter battles required by the topography. Sherman tanks couldn't break through the hedgerows. They could only roll over them, but that maneuver exposed the tanks' vulnerable underbellies to the German bazookas. Good old American ingenuity solved that problem. An inventive sergeant fabricated two steel beams and arrayed them like tusks on the prow of a tank, enabling the vehicle to remain on the ground while it punched through the hedgerows. Bradley characterized the innovation as "absurdly simple." The modification enabled the Shermans to effectively attack German positions in concert with accompanying infantry units.

Hampered by a lack of replacements, the German forces gave steady ground to the Allied invaders. On June 27th, Cherbourg fell to the Americans, giving the Allies control of their first real port. Montgomery and the British and Canadian forces were meeting with a series of frustrating counterattacks in their attempt to take Caen. Two major offensives had failed, and the British commander seemed content to remain locked in a battle of attrition with a German armored division.

While the Americans began to have doubts about their overall strategy, the Wehrmacht leaders were depressed by the amount of equipment, supplies and men being used up in the defense of their conquests in France. They knew that nothing they lost—not men, not equipment—could be replaced. Finally on July 12th, Caen fell, setting the stage for an Allied breakout from Normandy.

On July 25th, with most of Germany's tanks lured westward to deal with Montgomery's advance under Operation Goodwood, the Allies initiated Operation Cobra with a devastating air attack. The Americans faced a German front virtually bereft of armor, giving the GIs a clear advantage in their ability to utilize tank and infantry reinforcements, along with air power, to strike at any enemy in their path. This marriage of ground and air elements, while totally disheartening to the enemy, was not without its drawbacks. Botched bomb drops in friendly territory marred several missions, killing both Allied troops and French civilians. During Operation Cobra,

100 GI's were killed and 500 wounded by "friendly fire."

Although the combined strike force could be perilous for Allied soldiers when the advancing Allies closed to within 1,200 yards of the retreating Germans, the strategy nonetheless proved to be masterful. It allowed the U.S. First Army and Patton's newly formed Third Army to join in the advance toward Brittany after taking Avranches on July 30th. The plan was to make a left turn and encircle the Germans in Normandy from behind.

Hitler hated retreat of any kind, and he'd been experiencing a good deal of it on the eastern front as well. During the first half of 1944, the Russians were making steady advances and taking back their cities. The Soviet Union had one seemingly unlimited resource that Stalin was willing to sacrifice in the quest of victory—the Soviet people. Bolstered by the second fronts in North Africa and Italy—and now France—Stalin had been driving the Germans back toward their homeland for the past two years.

Hitler saw the Normandy breakout as a chance to establish another front. He hoped to drive around the American spearhead and reach the sea at Avranches. Once again, however, his plan was intercepted by Ultra, the allied intelligence system. As a result, the German operation *Luttich* was stopped in its tracks by heavy antitank defenses. With Allied reinforcements continuing to pour in and the Americans threatening to encircle German forces in Normandy, Hitler reluctantly approved the retreat on August 16th. Some 240,000 men, having abandoned most of their equipment, eventually fell back to the Seine River. They left behind some 50,000 dead and 200,000 taken prisoner.

The German High Command had been in crisis since Cherbourg had fallen in June. General Friedrich Dollman of the German Seventh Army, whose forces had failed on the Normandy beaches, died suddenly after the city's surrender. Death was supposedly caused by a heart attack, though Allied intelligence believed that Dollman had committed suicide. Rommel was attacked and severely injured on July 17th by a

British fighter. On July 2nd, the most devastating blow came when the German commander-in-chief of the western front, Field Marshall Gerd von Rundstedt, was relieved of duty after admitting to Hitler his defeatist views and urging the Fuhrer to make peace. Günther von Kluge, who soon came to share Rundstedt's sentiments, replaced him. On July 20th, a group of officers who saw the removal of Hitler as the only road to peace, made an attempt on the Fuhrer's life by planting a bomb at Hitler's East Prussian Headquarters in Rastenburg. A heavy wooden table reportedly cushioned Hitler from the explosion and led to the Fuhrer taking draconian powers over the army. Hitler also exacted revenge on anyone he suspected of opposing his views. Rommel, the most experienced of the German field generals, was forced to commit suicide in October to save the lives of his family members. Kluge killed himself on August 18th.

Field Marshal Walther Model, dubbed the "Fuhrer's fireman," succeeded Kluge. A veteran of the Russian front, where the German Army had become expert in the art of retreat, he was the architect of the Seine crossing. Model organized skillful rear-guard action operations to hold off the advancing Anglo-American forces from August 19th-31st while improvising pontoons and ferries to transport his men across the river that allied bombing had denuded of bridges. The Germans continued their retreat across northern France and into Belgium as resistance forces rose up in Paris against what remained of the German garrison in the city. As news of the struggle reached Eisenhower, he reversed his decision to bypass the City of Lights. Instead, Ike directed the recently arrived Free French Second Armored Division to liberate the city. On the morning of August 25, 1944, German commander Dietrich von Choltitz surrendered to Second Armored commander Philippe Leclerc. The next day, French General Charles de Gaulle led a victory parade down the Champs-Elysees to the Cathedral of Notre Dame, where a massive celebration ensued.

Capped by the liberation of Paris, the Normandy campaign had been a stunning military success. All but a small portion of France was under Allied control. American, British and Canadian forces now occupied Belgium and part of the Netherlands. By September, the Allies sat on the doorstep of the German frontier. They had, however, outrun their supply lines and now lacked the logistic support to mount a concluding offensive into the heart of the Fatherland. Before the supply crisis brought the allied offensive to a complete halt, Eisenhower made clearing the seaward approaches to Antwerp, located in Belgium on the English Channel, a priority. Use of this port would allow for a fresh transfusion of much-needed goods, mostly gasoline, to be brought in closer to where the troops were now fighting.

Eisenhower was convinced by Montgomery to back one bold attack aimed at taking advantage of the German disorganization before the Third Reich had a chance to regroup. Operation Market-Garden was to be a combination of air (Market)—utilizing the First Allied Airborne Army composed of one British and two American airborne divisions under Lt. General Lewis H. Brereton—and ground (Garden), involving the 2nd British Army under Montgomery. The operation's goal was to secure a workable bridgehead over the Rhine. This would pave the way for a British drive over the less fortified northern German Plain.

The surprise airdrop took place on September 17th, but the Germans reacted more quickly than expected. Stiff resistance limited Allied gains to a 50-mile front into Holland, far short of the objective. The Allies would have to be content with establishing a salient all along the German frontier as they waited to build up for the final assault that would put an end to the war in Europe.

Despite the setback of Market-Garden the Allies were confident that the war was about to reach a swift conclusion. As the Americans, British and Canadians approached from the west, the Russians were knocking on the Furher's eastern door. One final push and Berlin would fall long before winter set in. Hitler, however, had other ideas. As the Allies gathered their strength for a final push into the Fatherland, Hitler was formulating a desperate plan to crush the Allied invaders and save the Third Reich. He was massing his battered but battle-hardened forces for a ferocious counterattack designed to drive the Nazi Party's enemies back into the sea.

The most momentous clash in the history of warfare was about to begin—the Battle of the Bulge.

Army troops just prior to landing at
Normandy, June 6, 1944
(*Associated Press Photo*)

Rich Marowitz's intelligence and reconnaisance
(I & R) platoon. He is to the immediate right of the driver.

☆ ☆ ☆ ☆ ☆

Microphone in hand, Richard Marowitz is telling the students about service in an intelligence and reconnaissance platoon—about his precarious life as advance scout. An accomplished musician, magician and born showman—a man with a lifelong talent for capturing the attention of others and holding it—Marowitz speaks easily and authoritatively.

"It consisted of twenty-eight men," he's saying to the high school kids in the auditorium. "Four men to a Jeep, seven Jeeps. We usually worked in two squads—three Jeeps and twelve men each. The seventh Jeep was for the platoon leader. . . . We worked in two squads so we could cover more area, and we stayed in touch with radios, which worked sometimes—but not all the time. I was a scout on the point Jeep—which means that anytime we came to a clump of woods, a village or something that was suspicious, the scouts walked in . . . and cleared the area.

"And, if we didn't get killed, we waved the rest of the guys in. . . ."

RICHARD MAROWITZ

☆ ☆

Rich Marowitz had gifts. He had a feel for music, and he could always make people laugh—mainly because he found the world an endlessly entertaining and amusing place.

Born in Middletown, N.Y. in 1926, he moved at age 14 with his parents, Harry and Minnie, to a spacious three-bedroom apartment on Schenectady Avenue in Brooklyn. His father commuted to his coat factory in Jersey City, and his mother was a homemaker. His older brother, Sammy, who'd played in a swing band back in Middletown, introduced Marowitz to music. Less than a year after the family moved to Brooklyn, as Hitler was beginning his conquest of Europe, Marowitz found himself hanging out backstage at the Paramount in Manhattan and taking lessons from a trumpet and saxophone player named Claude Lackey. Sammy, who played with Lackey in the Harry James Band, had introduced them. Marowitz displayed a natural talent for music—and a passion for it.

Sammy, who was six years his senior, and Rich's sister, Roselyn, who was three years older than Sammy, had often told Marowitz that he could "read music before he was born." Marowitz also enjoyed a high energy level. As he took trumpet instruction, he also began studying conducting and arranging under a talented musician named Bill McGill.

"Bill was a genius," Marowitz recalled some 60 years later as he sat in his apartment in suburban Albany. "He was also an alcoholic. He lived somewhere on Eighth Avenue, not a very good section, in a one-room apartment. He had manuscript paper all over the floor, and he would just stand in the middle of this room and write. By the time he was done he had an arrangement for a 40-piece orchestra. There was a radio show back then called the 'Treasury Hour,' and he wrote the whole show."

At age 16, Marowitz heard Claude Lackey tell him, "There's nothing more I can teach you." Lackey sent the teenage trumpet player for more advanced instruction to Charlie Colin's studio on 48th Street. Studying and practicing three to four hours a day during the week and six or seven hours on the weekends did not make Marowitz popular with the other residents of his six-floor apartment building, but it wasn't long before Colin was hustling him down to the union hall, where Marowitz passed the test to earn his professional musician's license.

For the next two years, Marowitz played club dates in and around Manhattan and traveled the country with a swing band. Still in his teens, he was making $5,000 a year, roughly four times the income of the average American. He was dressing sharp and living well. His talent, discipline and maturity earned him the post of assistant bandleader, in charge of the other musicians, even though he was several years younger than most of them—which he pointedly did not divulge. While playing a date with the Ted Huston Band at the Plantation Club in Houston, Texas, Marowitz received an urgent message from Roselyn. Returning his older sister's call, he learned that the U.S. government was seeking the return of his draft questionnaire. Roselyn had mailed him the document while he was playing in Dallas. Where was it now, she wanted to know?

"It's probably in Dallas," Marowitz said, "but I'm in Houston. . . . And if you don't want your brother to end up in jail you'd better send me another one. Mail it to the Ainsley Hotel in Atlanta, Georgia."

Marowitz went on to Atlanta and called back to New

York for a trumpet player to replace him in the band. He'd been waiting for this. He was well aware that he was prime draft material and that his playing days were bound to be interrupted. Four days after returning his draft questionnaire, he boarded a train and headed home. He kept busy playing dates around New York City, but only two weeks passed before he was called for his draft physical. Two weeks after that, Richard Marowitz, swing band trumpeter, was Private Richard Marowitz, a member of the U.S. Army and on a bus to Fort Dix, N.J.

At Dix, the Army boxed up Marowitz's snappy civilian clothing and issued him a uniform. Marowitz spent the next 10 days undergoing processing and testing. At the end of the evaluation, he sat down with a sergeant who asked him what he wanted to do in the Army. High test scores had given Marowitz options. After learning that all the band positions had been filled, Marowitz offered to become a bugler—the only other duty available that was musically related.

"What no one bothered to tell me at the time," Marowitz recalled years later, "was that a bugler is also a message center runner and a scout. So, it was not a good idea."

Marowitz was assigned to basic training at what was considered the toughest training facility in the country—Camp Croft in Spartanburg, S.C. Unbeknownst at the time to Marowitz and his fellow inductees, Camp Croft had recently slipped to third place in the Army's basic training ratings, and the camp commander had every intention of lifting Croft back to its previous stature. The facility was earning a reputation more for burning men out than building them up. All Rich Marowitz knew was that his bony, 5-foot 9 1/2-inch, 125-pound, 18-year-old body now belonged to Uncle Sam. Camp Croft instructors were charged with quickly turning him and his fellow draftees into fighting men. The great invasion was underway; American blood was spilling on European soil.

The 16,929-acre facility had been completed on May 15, 1941 after only 154 days of construction. It could house as many as 20,000 trainees and was also home to 500 German prisoners of war taken during the North Africa campaign, who were put to work on local farms. In addition to barracks and headquarters buildings, Camp Croft boasted a post office, movie theaters, chapels, dental clinics, service clubs, a hospital, 19.5 miles of paved roadways and pumping and sewage facilities. It was named for a Greenville, S.C. native, Major General Edward Croft; a former U.S. Army Chief of Infantry who'd died in 1938. The $10.3 million project had been the largest in the history of the area, providing work for 12,000 men in a region hit especially hard by the Great Depression. It had been located in South Carolina largely through the influence of U.S. Sen. James F. Byrnes, a Spartanburg resident.

June 1944 was a steamy month in South Carolina. Temperatures routinely soared to over 100 degrees in the shade. Buglers were considered specialists, as opposed to ordinary infantrymen. For them, basic consisted of seven weeks of accelerated infantry training followed by seven weeks of schooling in the use of the 300 and 694 radio and the code converter. That was followed by two weeks of field maneuvers and one week of testing.

For Marowitz, a typical day consisted of falling out at 5 AM and running a mile to the obstacle course. Trainees were required to complete the course route twice—jumping over logs, crawling under logs, running cross-country through streams and scrambling over a 10-foot wall. The first time he saw the wall and realized that he was expected to climb it, Marowitz said, "That is not possible."

The drill sergeant responded, "You dumb bastard, you run at that wall full speed, hit it with your toe and push yourself up and grab the top with your fingertips, and then pull yourself up and swing your leg over and fall down on the other side."

Marowitz gave it a shot. Running at top speed, he slammed into the wall and bounced off. The sergeant was laughing. Marowitz was not.

"I got so damn mad," he recalled years later. "Once I finally did it, I could do it every time. I was going over that wall like a damn fly."

After finishing the obstacle course a second time, the recruits would run back to camp for breakfast. From there, as temperatures began to soar, it was on to the water fountain, next to which was stationed a large container of salt tablets. The men would drink as much as they could hold and grab a handful of pills. They knew that was all the water they would see until noon.

"They wanted to teach us water discipline," Marowitz recalled. "Damn stupid; you'd never see that nowadays."

Next came bayonet drill. Troops would face a dummy flanked by sticks on each side. Troops would parry left or parry right, depending on the orders bellowed out by the instructor. The object of the exercise was for the trainee to get his bayonet in and out of the dummy before the stick swung around and hit him. Yelling with every thrust, the trainees would drill with the bayonets and dummies until noon. By then, they were exhausted and hoarse.

After the morning session, the men would line up and hold their canteens at arm's length. A lieutenant would walk up and down the line as each man, in turn, was allowed a single swallow. The troops then were directed to pour the rest of the canteen's contents on the ground. No more water was allowed until afternoon training ended. As sweat poured from them in torrents, the troops moved on to the firing range and then to village fighting instruction or infiltration. During infiltration drills, recruits were required to crawl through the mud, over and under barbed wire, as live tracers whizzed over their backs.

"That was crappy stuff," Marowitz remembered. "They liked to run those exercises at night and scare the hell out of us. In the dark, it seemed like those tracers were right on top of us."

At the end of the seven weeks, most men with specialist designations were relieved to have completed basic training. Unfortunately, Marowitz and his fellow specialists would attend only one week of school before the company commander informed them that, due to the shortage of regular riflemen overseas, school was suspended, and everyone would have to start basic all over again. The commander told them that weekend passes would be issued, and drills would resume on Tuesday—for an additional seven weeks.

"A lot of guys wanted to go over the hill," Marowitz recounted decades later, "but no one did."

After another seven weeks of basic training and two weeks of maneuvers in the woods—including the customary 25-mile hike in full equipment—the troops underwent physical testing. Tanned and his hair close-cropped, Marowitz had put on 20 pounds of muscle. The transformation was so stark that when his parents came to visit, Minnie Marowitz walked right past her son without recognizing him.

"I was hard as a rock," Marowitz recalled. "If you touched me with your finger, it broke. It was the craziest thing. Guys who came in heavy lost weight and guys like me gained it."

The America of the 1940s consisted of more or less isolated regions, each with its own distinct culture. One of the buddies Marowitz made at Camp Croft was from Birmingham, Alabama. The man was astonished to discover that Marowitz was Jewish. He'd never before met a Jew.

"You're a great guy," the buddy said. "I can't believe it."

Marowitz replied, "Look, I've got short hair, no horns. See, there's not a hell of lot of difference between us."

The two men remained friends throughout basic, but Marowitz's buddy couldn't wait for his wife to visit Camp Croft so she could meet his Jewish friend.

"He wound up going to the Rainbow like me," Marowitz said nearly 60 years later. "He ended up being sent back from overseas on a section eight."

At the end of basic training, Marowitz was given 11 days to report to Camp Gruber in Braggs, Oklahoma. After spending a week at home, he found himself waiting at Grand Central Station with his mother and father. Nearby was another young soldier, who was at least a head shorter than Marowitz and was also with his parents. The two families began chatting. Once they realized that both young soldiers were reporting to camp in Ok., the mother of the young man, whom Marowitz would end up calling Swartzey, asked him if he would take care of her son. Marowitz assured her he would.

Years later he recalled, "She must have thought I was older, even though we were the same age—although I had had a different kind of experience starting at age 16. What she said kind of struck me, so I tried to keep track of him. I ran into him a couple of times at camp, but he was assigned to an infantry company, and he was killed two weeks after going into combat."

☆ ☆ ☆

Pulling into the train station at Braggs, Oklahoma in early September 1944, New York-bred Richard Marowitz had to look twice to even spot the town, whose entire population totaled 308 souls. In Europe, Allied forces were pushing the Germans across France and back into the Dragon's Teeth. Fierce fighting still raged in the jungle islands of the Pacific and in the mountains of Italy. Once through basic training every GI's mind was focused on where he might end up.

Camp Gruber was adjacent to Braggs in east-central Oklahoma in Muskogee County. The largest town in the region was Muskogee, population 37,700, located about 10 miles west of the installation. Marowitz was part of the of the reactivation of the 42nd Infantry, the legendary Rainbow Division, made famous in World War I for 174 straight days of combat and for incurring every 16th casualty suffered by American forces during that conflict. In memory of their fallen comrades, surviving members of the 42nd had ripped their rainbow patches in half before leaving France, leaving the unit with a half-rainbow as its emblem.

The Rainbow Division had been deactivated after the first great war. Now it was back, occupying a 67,638-acre camp with 2,200 buildings that had opened on May 15, 1942. Like

Camp Croft, Camp Gruber also served as a prisoner of war containment facility, housing some 3,000 of Rommel's Afrika Corps who were put to work in the local community. When leaving Camp Croft, Marowitz had been reassigned as an infantry rifleman. Upon reaching Camp Gruber, however, he was reinstated as a bugler and found himself attached to headquarters company of the 222nd Infantry regiment, although he'd completed none of the required training. The previous company bugler had been deemed unfit for overseas duty.

Marowitz was to report to the recreation hall and see a Corporal Stippy, who was in charge of the bugle corp. On the way, Marowitz passed a captain, whom he saluted. The captain proceeded to ream him out.

"What the hell's the matter with you, soldier?" the captain demanded. "Did you forget your salute already?"

Mystified, Marowitz explained that he'd saluted as he'd been taught. The exasperated captain ordered him back to the command post for instruction in the proper Rainbow salute. Reporting to the first sergeant, Marowitz recounted his run-in with the officer. The sergeant explained that the Rainbow was the only U.S. Army division authorized its own special salute.

"He was laughing," Marowitz recalled years later. "The first thing you do is look up to the sky, like you're looking for a rainbow as you salute, and your hand arcs like a rainbow on the way down. And, at the same time, you click your heels together. When he taught me, I thought to myself that I'm in the German army, and I don't know it."

Armed with the proper salutation, Marowitz finally managed to report to Corporal Stippy, who handed him a plastic bugle. Stippy asked Marowitz if he'd ever blown a bugle. Marowitz produced a small leather case, one he would carry with him throughout the war, and pulled out the mouthpiece to his trumpet. Marowitz inserted the mouthpiece into the plastic bugle. No, he told the corporal, he'd never blown a bugle.

Stippy then asked if he wanted to be shown how to play the horn. Just hum a bugle call, Marowitz suggested. The corporal complied. Marowitz then put the bugle to his lips and blasted out the call with the panache of the professional he was.

"Oh, my god," the corporal said. "Where'd you learn to play like that?"

Marowitz explained his background and was immediately made "bugler of the guard." Stationed at the guardhouse on 24-hour duty, Marowitz was required to play some 20 calls a day. He had his parents send his trumpet to him.

"The plastic bugle was a pain in the ass," Marowitz remembered years later. "I started using the trumpet, and word spread quickly. Guys were coming up to me and saying they would stay up just to hear me play. I got in a little trouble one day with a captain who accused me of jazzing up the calls, which I did. Corporal Stippy told him that I was the most accomplished bugler we ever had, but that didn't satisfy him. Finally, I made up a story about how it was cold, and my trumpet was cold, and sometimes it cracks like your voice. He half accepted the story and stormed out. Stippy told me I had a lot of guts talking to him like that. I said, 'What's he gonna do? Fire me?'"

When he wasn't jazzing up his bugle calls, Marowitz packed ordinance. Orders had come down in October that the men of the Rainbow would be shipping out soon, but no one knew where or when they would go. Captain John McLaughlin was commanding officer of headquarters company and was well liked by everyone under his authority. Always eager to help, he would ferry enlisted men to town and back to base when they had passes.

Their first meeting came one morning when Marowitz was summoned to the command post to find the captain waiting. The officer took Marowitz to the motor pool, where equipment was being crated for shipment. Around 8 AM, the captain ordered a lieutenant to instruct Marowitz on packaging the equipment and labeling the containers. The captain informed Marowitz that he was in charge of the area and would be pulling an eight-hour shift. At the end of the work period, Marowitz sought out the lieutenant in search of a replacement. I'll be right back, the lieutenant said—and promptly disappeared.

Eight hours later, a new lieutenant came on duty. Seeking relief after a 16-hour shift, Marowitz told the new lieutenant what had happened. I'll take care of it, the lieutenant said—only he didn't. Eight hours later, the captain returned, saw Marowitz still on the job and asked him what was going on. After listening to Marowitz's explanation, McLaughlin sought out the original lieutenant and handed him Marowitz's clip board.

"This kid has been here for 24 hours," Captain McLaughlin told the lieutenant. "You couldn't find a replacement, so *you* finish the job."

Motioning Marowitz to get in the Jeep, the captain drove him back to the command post and ordered him to go upstairs and get some sleep. Captain McLaughlin then instructed the sergeant to issue Marowitz a three-day pass. Marowitz expressed his gratitude.

"It's okay," the officer replied. "You earned it."

Marowitz had made a friend with bars on his shoulder. It was, he would discover later, a friendship that would put Richard Marowitz's life at serious risk.

On November 11th, the men at Camp Gruber were restricted to base. The GI's understood that the moment had arrived; they finally were going to war. The soldiers waited restlessly, watched movies or wrote their families, wondering where they would be sent. Long trains of Pullman cars and troop sleepers began forming near the shacks of Braggs. Two days later, Marowitz and the 222nd infantry regiment, along with the 232nd and 242nd—known collectively as Task Force Linden—boarded the train as the division band played the "Rainbow Song" and "Mountain Dew." Despite all attempts at secrecy, everyone understood that their intermediate destination of Camp Kilmer, N.J. meant that they likely were heading to Europe. Most figured that the Third Reich was finished and that the Rainbow would end up as an occupation force. No one on the train imagined what really lay ahead.

On November 25th, Richard Marowitz and the thousands of other novice fighting men of the reconstituted Rainbow Division boarded the olive drab *SS America* for the surprisingly comfortable voyage to France. After a week of losing their lunches overboard and then getting their sea legs, the troops finally settled into the routine of their 15-day sea journey. Once they adapted, there were movies, a library, language classes, ample chow of a higher-than-expected quality, abandon ship drills and ample companionship to pass the time.

In addition to the routine on-board activities, Marowitz followed his natural instinct to entertain. Exploring the ship, he located a glass enclosure in the vessel's ballroom containing a control room and enough records to enable him to broadcast music throughout the *SS America*. After convincing a lieutenant to permit the activity, Marowitz became the ship's disk jockey for the trip's duration.

"The way it was set up," Marowitz recalled, "I could speak to any deck or portion of a deck. I had nothing else to do, so I got up early and worked 'til late at night. I played music, told jokes and just screwed around. The guys were so hungry that they'd listen to anything. Whatever I did was okay. If I told the same joke 20 times it didn't matter; they'd laugh anyway."

Sailing down the Mediterranean, in sight of the coast of Africa, the ship was abuzz with rumors of Italy as a potential destination. But on the misty morning of December 9, 1944 the ship entered a harbor between the gleaming yellow cliffs that towered over the port town of Marseilles.

That afternoon, the young men of the Rainbow Division debarked the *SS America*. They found the Old World city of Marseilles a far cry from home. They were accosted on the squalid streets by beggars who understood that the best time to relieve a soldier of cigarettes and chocolates was when his feet first hit French soil. In time, the GI's would grow accustomed to this ritual and find it easier to refuse the beggar who always demanded more, no matter what was offered. The newly minted American soldiers strode along the fish-reeking waterfront, past a large submarine base built by the Nazis that now housed German prisoners of war. Richard Marowitz and his comrades lounged in a large open area and waited for the trucks that would whisk them through the winding roads of the city and up into the hill country.

Toward the scene of what would become the Battle of the Bulge.

The "Dragon's Teeth" from the air
(*Associated Press Photo*)

"Nuts!"

☆ ☆

—General Anthony McAuliffe's one-word answer to the
Germans who called for his surrender at Bastogne.

As 1944 wound down, the jaws of the Allied armies
were closing on Germany.

The Russians lurked along the Vistula River and the
borders of East Prussia. The British and Americans were
poised along the several hundred miles of German border
known as the Sigfried Line—a zone of fortifications constructed before the German invasion of France in 1940. The fortified
line was named after a legendary hero who'd killed the Dragon
Fafnir. It consisted, in part, of fields of chest-high concrete pyr-
amids, planted side by side in the Earth. They were designed
to stop tanks. In keeping with the Sigfried myth, the tank bar-
rier thrusting up along the German border was called The
Dragon's Teeth.

Months earlier, after the Allies had swept ashore at
Normandy, Hitler had come to accept the annihilation of his
forces on the Eastern Front. Instead of bolstering their numbers, he diverted resources to battle the Anglo-American forces
driving his armies across France toward the Sigfried Line. But
the German effort on the Western Front was failing. By year's
end the Allied commanders concluded that they had seen the
last of any meaningful German resistance. Hitler, however,
had other plans. He was massing his forces to launch an all-or-

nothing counterattack through the dense Ardennes Forest—a sprawling, tree-studded plateau of more than 2,000 square miles in northeastern France, southeastern Belgium and Luxembourg.

That summer, Hitler had begun building a large reserve force composed primarily of conscripted teenagers, old men and those previously deemed unfit for service. Despite the beating Germany was taking on both fronts, Hitler had no intention of using this new resource to bolster his existing forces. The newly formed "people's army" was led by veteran commanders who hoped that outfitting these divisions with more automatic weapons and supplying them with extra supporting artillery, such as assault guns and rocket battalions, would compensate for their paucity of proper training. In addition to creating the new people's army, Hitler also rebuilt his Panzer divisions—tank troops—with survivors of the bloodletting at Normandy and on the Eastern Front.

Operation *Wacht Am Rhine* (Watch on the Rhine) was a high-risk mission focused on the capture of the port of Antwerp, Belgium. Hitler's intention was to mass 25 divisions for an attack aimed at what he perceived to be the Allies' weak point in the Ardennes. His plan called for his army to overwhelm the thinly guarded American salient, make its way across the Meuse River and then turn and plow northwest some 60 miles to Antwerp. He hoped to sever the Allied supply lines in the north and to surround and destroy up to a third of the Allied ground forces. Hitler believed that such an assault would smash the unity of the Allied coalition by greatly crippling their ground forces. This would allow him time to deal with the Russians on Germany's eastern doorstep and leave the Nazis in a stronger position, if necessary, to negotiate favorable terms for a peace.

Hitler knew that his plan had no chance unless he neutralized Allied air power, so part of his strategy was to delay the attack until inclement weather would ground allied planes. The few German generals he still trusted expressed unease over the proposed operation's massive scope. Field Marshal

Gerd von Rundstedt, commander-in-chief of the German forces in the west, and Army Group B Commander Walter Model, the two men in charge of the operation, feared that their armies no longer possessed sufficient tank and aerial fire-power to conduct a successful blitzkrieg. In addition, the newly conscripted infantry soldiers were well below the standards of troops the Germans had begun the war with. Moreover, supply lines would be imperiled by a shoddy system of roads in the Ardennes. To Rundstedt and Model, the plan contained too many variables. They also were unconvinced that a successful *Wacht Am Rhine* would drive a wedge between the British and Americans.

The pessimism of the German commanders was rooted in their realization that the Ardennes terrain was distinctly daunting. The area consisted of a series of parallel ridges and valleys running from northeast to southwest. One third of the region was covered by dense coniferous forest and narrow, deep gorges where countless streams and rivers intersected the ridges. To the north lay swamps and marshland. With only a few good roads, movement in the central sector would be difficult until the ground froze. Before that, vehicles could easily become mired in the mud of fall rain or early winter snows. It would be necessary for the Germans to reach the road centers of Bastogne and Houffalize in the south and Malmedy and St. Vith in the north before they could manage an effective military breakout through the Ardennes. Once across the Meuse River, however, the path to Antwerp consisted of good roads and few obstructions. The best argument for Hitler's plan was that the assault route was so irrational that the Allies surely would be caught off guard.

In fact, General Dwight D. Eisenhower, the supreme Allied commander, had positioned his forces where terrain was better suited for an advance into Germany than a defense against a German counterattack. British Field Marshal Bernard Montgomery's 21st Army Group was far north of the Ardennes sector. Lt. General Omar N. Bradley's 12th Army Group was located to the south. Lt. General Jacob L. Dever's Sixth Army

Group was still further south and west of Bradley in the Alsace region. All were preparing for a foray across the Rhine in early 1945.

The Ardennes located in the center of Bradley's sector had been classified as a "ghost front" with no appreciable activity since mid-September. The 12th Army Group's deployment reflected those perceptions as Lt. General William H. Simpson's Ninth Army and the majority of Lt. General Courtney H. Hodges First Army were stationed 40 miles north of the Ardennes awaiting orders to invade the Ruhr region. Lt. General George S. Patton, Jr., Eisenhower's ferocious tank commander, was in position for a thrust into the essential Saar mining region, a 100 miles south of the forest. In between, four remaining divisions—two with no combat experience and two veteran units convalescing from bitter battles in the Hurtgen Forest—were left, along with an armored infantry battalion and two cavalry squadrons, to cover 88 miles of front.

Despite reports from civilians about a German build-up in the area, Allied intelligence mistakenly judged the Germans too weak to mount an offensive. Intelligence experts concluded that Hitler was moving troops only to thwart an allied invasion into the Ruhr and the Saar regions. Bad weather had made air reconnaissance and photography useless. Hitler's growing suspicions about the loyalty of his own staff had prompted him to keep communication to a minimum. The lack of meaningful German radio transmissions to intercept and interpret left the Allied command with a false sense of security. A lack of radio chatter confirmed their erroneous belief that nothing was happening. Hitler's paranoia turned out to be his best security for the operation.

The need for speed and power during the attack prompted Hitler to combine four SS Panzer divisions into one concentrated Sixth Panzer Army. Led by Lt. General Josef "Sepp" Dietrich, they would bear the main burden in Field Marshal Model's attack, code named *Herbstnebel* (Autumn Fog). They would engage Hodges' First Army in the northern Ardennes with the intent of overrunning their 99th infantry division before driving for the Meuse River and Antwerp. Attacking the center of the Allied lines would be the newly formed Fifth Panzer Army led by Lt. General Hasso von Manteuffel as a secondary effort with the same objective. Just south of Manteuffel would be the German Seventh Army, led by Lt. General Erich Brandenberger, whose assignment was to engage and then cover the advance of the Panzers as far as the Meuse River. To the north of Dietrich's Sixth Panzer Army was the 15th Army, led by General Gustav von Zangen, whose two-fold mission was to use his six divisions to pin down the Americans in the Aachen sector and then attack southward after the Sixth Panzer had broken the American salient. To add to the chaos, an airborne drop behind Allied lines of small groups of English-speaking Germans in American uniforms was scheduled.

During the days before the attack in mid-December, Hitler had managed to amass a force of some 30 divisions and 1,500 planes in the Eifel. In the Ardennes, his forces would enjoy an overall 3-to-1 numerical advantage and an edge of 10-to-1 at the point of engagement. The German troops were well armed. Most of them had sprung from the Hitler Youth. They had, in essence, been raised by the Nazis for such an event, and they had been cunningly roused to a fever's pitch to serve both their Fuhrer and the Fatherland.

Opposing the German assault on the other side of the Eifel would be the battle-weary Second Infantry Division, which had suffered so many casualties that it contained more replacements than veterans, although the division's core of experienced company commanders remained intact. The 99th and 106th Divisions, who were relatively green combat units but had spent enough time on the front to be useful, attended the line to the right of the Second Division. Most of their rifle-men had only been partially trained. The winter was rapidly becoming one of the coldest in 30 years. Overcast, snowy days were made even more miserable by the fact that the Allied infantry was short of food. Because no fires could be lit, none of the food available could be consumed hot. Most GI's had to eat snow because their canteens were empty. The lack of proper winter clothing meant they spent most of the time shivering in their foxholes. The bitter weather in the Ardennes would inflict heavy casualties through frostbite, pneumonia and trench foot—taking out four times as many Allied soldiers as German bombs, bullets and artillery shells.

Despite the hugh German manpower advantage over the Allied troops in the Ardennes, the Allies had more big guns and aircraft. In addition, the Allied roadway transportation system was far superior to the German railway system for moving war materiel and sustaining the supply lines crucial to any successful military campaign. Hitler would need to launch a speedy surprise attack that would sow panic in the Allied ranks and force retreat—if the Germans were lucky enough to see only a slow response from Allied command. To guarantee that speed, the Germans would have to rely on capturing American stocks, especially gasoline. All this in concert with a prolonged stretch of bad weather to keep the dominant Allied air force grounded made for a perilous gamble. Hitler, however, despite the best advice from his staff to shorten the scope of the operation, believed that the Germans remained a vastly superior fighting force to what he judged to be the inexperienced, poorly motivated Americans. Convinced that German defeats since D-Day had been due only to Allied air superiority—and positive that the bad weather would keep most Allied planes out of the sky during this operation—the Fuhrer was willing to roll the dice.

As the German army attacked the American salient in the Ardennes on the morning of December 16, 1944, weather conditions were nearly perfect for the success of Hitler's plan. A misty snow was falling on the already snow-carpeted ground. Fog shrouded the massive German force of vehicles and exquisitely uniformed troops carrying new automatic weapons. Morale was sky high. The day marked the first in months that German troops were moving forward instead of backtracking. Both German combat veterans and untested replacements felt a soaring sense of enthusiasm.

Just before the sun rose on December 16th in the Ardennes, the ground began to shake as V-1 rockets, heavy artillery and mortar fire pounded U.S. positions with coordinated precision. The bombardment lasted a little over an hour. It was followed by waves of German troops swarming into the area. They were led by an Eastern Front veteran, Lt. Colonel Jochen Peiper. He was a highly regarded, single-minded leader whom Hitler counted on to set the pace in leading the pack to the Meuse River. Peiper's SS First Panzer Division consisted of a huge force of 22,000 men, 250 tanks and two companies of engineers. His sole objective was to reach the river, and advance more than 80 kilometers by day's end over roads designed for bicycles rather than tanks.

Initially, Allied infantry troops thought that the unexpected bombardment was firepower from American guns. They soon grasped the truth and scampered into foxholes to huddle, perplexed and confused.

The largest and most important battle in U.S. history was underway.

This map shows the German lines surrounding
Bastogne, Belgium, where the Americans were located

THE BULGE

☆ ☆

While the Germans had achieved the element of surprise in optimal conditions for their offensive, what Hitler was
counting on most did not happen. American soldiers, many
seeing combat for the first time, did not retreat in panic.
Initially, most held their ground and continued to fight in small
groups, holding the few roads available for the German
advance and delaying Hitler's objective of reaching the Meuse
that first day. The Germans made a tactical error by having
their infantry lead the artillery instead of moving in unison.
That enabled the GI's to hold them off that first day. While the
Germans managed to break through the American lines with
hundreds of tanks moving freely behind the American salient,
the German counteroffensive was critically behind schedule.
As darkness fell that first night on December 16th, the Fifth
Panzer Division and German Seventh Army had failed to penetrate the American line.

When news of the enemy attack reached Allied
Command Headquarters that first night, Eisenhower was celebrating his promotion to five-star general as his friend and 12th
Army General Omar Bradley arrived. Bradley viewed the
attack as a mere irritant, but Ike disagreed. He concluded that
the Allies were facing a major counteroffensive and quickly
began reassigning his troops. Studying his maps, Eisenhower
shifted his forces from preparing to attack into Germany to
defending the Ardennes. Among his realignment directives,

he sent the 101st to Bastogne, a crossroads town in the middle of the German advance. Eisenhower ordered Bastogne defended at all costs.

By December 17th, he'd redirected the priorities of the Red Ball Express. Now, instead of carrying supplies, the trucks were moving troops. More than 10,000 trucks moved 60,000 men into the Ardennes in a single day. In a week's time, Eisenhower was able to deploy more than 250,000 troops and 50,000 fighting vehicles to repel the attack. The Allied army was displaying a degree of mobility never before seen. The allies resorted to extreme measures to obtain bodies to enlarge their fighting force. Any soldier able to walk was ordered out of his hospital bed and sent back to the retrenching front.

Hitler was reportedly ecstatic with the *Wacht Am Rhine* operation after the first day. He had no clue that the Americans would move so quickly to quell his offensive. Having ordered the bombing of Allied communication lines before the attack, Hitler had imagined it would take several days before Eisenhower and his staff would grasp the scale of the maneuver. Only spotty radio transmission would be available to the Allies in that rugged terrain. Once the Allies figured out the scope of his attack, Hitler speculated, it would still take another few days before a bureaucratic committee of senior Allied commanders could decide on a course of action. By then, the Germans would have split the U.S. and British forces and captured Antwerp.

Hitler had not anticipated that Eisenhower would recognize the threat and initiate such a lightning-fast response. The Fuhrer's misjudgment of Eisenhower's perception and adaptability simply added to the laundry list of things that could—and did—go wrong with the Nazi execution of the operation. Hitler had failed to anticipate that Eisenhower would view the attack not just as a threat but also a golden opportunity for the Allies. Hitler's boldness permitted the Allies to engage the Germans in the open—not while Nazi forces were hunkered down in defensive positions behind the fortifications of the Siegfried Line. *Wacht Am Rhine* also exposed nearly all the remaining German reserves. As the battle raged, Eisenhower felt that Hitler's predisposition to attack rather than defend would hasten the end of the war in Europe.

The badly undermanned Luftwaffe flew its last significant mission of the war on December 17th in the skies over Belgium. German pilots managed between 600 and 700 sorties in support of their infantry despite the 1,000 or more Allied planes that intercepted them in a day-long aerial dogfight over St. Vith. With the cloud ceiling at 5,000 feet, the 17th was one of very few days during the first two weeks of the battle when aircraft could be effective.

As Hitler's generals had warned, the Germans were beginning to bog down on the substandard Ardennes roads. Traffic jams were common. Because of a shortage of gasoline and trucks, most German infantrymen were on foot. Most artillery pieces were pulled by horses. Nonetheless, by the evening of the 17th, the Fifth Panzer Division had made its major breakthrough in the center of the American line and moved in the direction of Bastogne. Moreover, Peiper—with his SS First Panzer Division in the north—was clearly the major problem facing the Allies. If he crossed the Meuse River, Peiper would have a clear road to Antwerp.

In the 36 hours since the initial attack, Peiper had managed to get as far as the village of Stavelot, where he was met by stiff American resistance. Along the way, he'd captured and murdered more than 300 POW's and 100 Belgian civilians at a dozen locations, slaughtering 80 alone just southeast of Malmedy. It was Peiper's view that his imperative to move with lightning speed meant he could take no prisoners. He realized, however—after his cruel treatment of the people he'd captured—that he and his men were likely to meet with the same grisly fate were they captured. As word spread of the "Malmedy Massacre," American resolve stiffened. Peiper was well behind schedule by dawn of the 18th when he launched an attack that drove defending Americans from Stavelot, but the GI's destroyed their gasoline stores as they left. Frustrated at his inability to procure precious fuel, Peiper sped toward

Trois-Ponts (three bridges) hoping to find an intact route across the river.

Under heavy pressure from German forces, the trickle of shocked American soldiers in retreat was now increasing to a torrent. By the end of December 17th, steady lines of GI's leaving the front finally developed into a panicked and disorganized procession. By the next day, the Germans had begun to figure out their traffic issues and were gaining momentum. As word of the invasion spread, French and Belgian citizens prepared for the return of the Germans. In the United States, the stock market rallied in response to an extension of the conflict. On December 19th, as the 101st Airborne Division arrived in Bastogne, columns of retreating soldiers who'd left behind artillery, jeeps and rations were passing on whatever ammo or weapons they had to fresh troops heading toward the front. The retreating Allied forces were creating road congestion problems as they intersected with men and vehicles heading toward the battle. In spite of the retreat, many pockets of resistance still held their ground as they cut down the inexperienced infantrymen the Nazis had plucked from the ranks of the Hitler Youth and rushed into combat for this operation. Teenagers were killing teenagers. Each side was finishing this hellish conflict with children doing the fighting.

As Eisenhower met with his staff at dawn on December 19th, he remained upbeat as he saw what the Allies were already calling the "Bulge" as an opportunity for his army. Patton pointed out that the Germans were putting themselves in position to be cut off from their supply lines and destroyed. Patton wanted to move his Third Army north and isolate the German tanks inside the Bulge. When asked how long it would take him to move his corps, Patton said two days. The other generals laughed, but Patton's men were already implementing his strategy. As the meeting's mood turned truly positive, German tanks were surrounding the 101st Airborne at Bastogne.

Fierce fighting was taking place all along the retrenching American salient, where the Allies had surrendered most of their ground at the center and to Peiper's spearhead in the North. Critical road junctions at St. Vith and Bastogne were under siege but were being defended by the 82nd and 101st respectively. Fearful of a lengthy confrontation, some German Army units had opted to bypass these crucial intersections in favor of continuing the push for the Meuse River. With limited effective routes available, they would be moving directly into the face of the American reinforcements pouring into the conflict.

The Battle of the Bulge was in full flame, and neither side could predict its outcome.

The M4-A1 Sherman Tank
(*Associated Press Photo*)

The three veterans are taking turns at the microphone. It's Doug Vink's turn again. He stands, takes the mike and gazes out at the students.

"Every day," he's saying, "it was anywhere from thirty to 40 below zero. Every day. It was so overcast that our aircraft could not get up at all to give us a hand with anything. The winds would be forty, fifty miles an hour. How the infantry guys ever stood it, I don't know. We were cold enough in those tanks. Of course, everybody thought we had heaters, but there were no heaters, no air conditioning like there is today in tanks. . . .

"I was in what was known as the M4-A1 Sherman tank, a medium tank—seventy five milimeter gun, a thirty caliber machine gun mounted right next to it, a fifty caliber machine gun mounted on the top. And where the assistant driver sat, there was a bow gun. That was a thirty caliber machine gun. That would move back and forth and up and down only fifteen degrees, so he had to be facing everybody that he shot at. . . .

"We could not take a German tank head on. Our shells would just bounce off the German tanks. When they fired at us, they could hit us anyplace. Our tanks got to be known as the Ronson lighters because as soon as one got hit, it went right up in flames. If you got out, you were lucky. The only way we got them was to have two or three tanks firing at them to distract them. Then a couple tanks would go around behind them or beside them. And that's the only way we could knock off those tanks. . . ."

Doug Vink

Doug Vink

☆ ☆

In December 1944, northern Europe was shrouded in thick clouds of battleship gray. By this time, after six months on the front lines, Doug Vink was used to being shot at. It occurred almost daily. His outfit had been in the thick of fighting fairly steadily since leaving Lorrient, where they'd been relieved by an infantry outfit. Every day, the Allies had moved forward, inch by inch, taking ground, pushing the Germans back toward the Fatherland.

Despite the shells bursting around him, Vink remained optimistic. The Germans clearly were on the run. In a letter home to a sister, he'd written a poem entitled, "We'll All Come Back." It read:

> *The time has been long, the fighting rough,*
> *But all our boys are hard and tough,*
> *They fear not a man and bat not an eye*
> *They're fighting to preserve a home, for just you and I.*
> *They'll do it, too, if we give them time;*
> *We'll fight up to the last drop of blood,*
> *In sunshine, rain or mud.*
> *We'll make the paper hanger pay his debt,*
> *Just wait and see; we're not finished with him yet.*
> *And when we are, each mother will see her son,*
> *They'll be coming home, one by one,*
> *We're all coming back, as I said before,*
> *Only a few will now be missing from the score,*
> *And even those who are left behind,*

will come back to life in someone's mind,
Do you see, Sis, what I've just told you,
Will eventually all turn out true,
We're coming back to our homes so dear,
And then and only then can we all share
The love and happiness of those so near,
We're coming back to those we love,
We're coming back, I know,
'cause it's been written in the books above.

Then, on December 16th, came the counterattack, and
everything changed. Eisenhower met with his generals at
Verdun, trying to figure out how to counter the German offensive. Ike's tank boss, Gen. George S. Patton, with typical confidence and aplomb, offered to take an armored division and
two infantry divisions and break through to Bastogne, where
Germans had American forces surrounded. After gathering
his forces, Patton began rolling December 22, 1944.

Moving in tandem with the 35th Infantry Division,
Vink's Sixth Armored was crawling along the shores of the
Sahr River in Luxembourg near the German border when
orders came for the outfit to move toward Metz. Patton was
calling on them to fight at Bastogne. The tanks began rolling
with a rumble of internal combustion, grinding gears and
heavy, clanking steel tracks. Each company in the division had
18 tanks. Each platoon had five.

Ernest Hemingway, in his introduction to a collection of
war stories, expressed the view that tank warfare—for all its
dependence on steel, gears and mechanics—represented not a
clash of technology but, at its core, basic combat between
human beings. Hemingway wrote, ". . . a horse will carry a
man in his first action where his legs might not go; and a mechanized vehicle will carry him further than a horse will go; but
finally no mechanized vehicle is any better than the heart of the
man who handles the controls."

As they moved toward Metz, resistance was immediately stiff. From his slot in the tank, Vink could see German
tanks in the distance surrounded by infantry. The Shermans

were no match for the larger, more heavily armed and armored German Panzers and Tigers, and their commanders knew it. The Sherman's 75 MM cannon could penetrate 3.7 inches of armor plating at 500 yards. Unfortunately, the most lightly armored German tank, the Tiger, had frontal armor four inches thick. The Panzer IV, generally viewed as the weakest German tank overall, nonetheless boasted 4.8 inches of frontal armor plating. Moreover, each German tank possessed an 88 MM cannon that could punch effortlessly through the Sherman's armor even at great distances.

The Sherman, however, was simpler in design than either the Panzer or the Tiger, which made it easier and cheaper to manufacture and less prone to mechanical failure. Ultimately, 11 factories operating at full production turned out nearly 50,000 Shermans in just a few years, more tanks than the Third Reich had been able to turn out during its build-up years before the war or during the war itself. That was, however, a command-level strategic procurement consideration that meant little to the tank crews who actually had to go into combat with the lighter Shermans against the burlier Panzers and Tigers.

Consequently, Sherman commanders avoided frontal combat with the larger, more potent German fighting machines. The preferred method of combat for the Sad Sack and the other American tanks was to move out of the way of a Panzer or Tiger, maneuver to the side and try to fire a killing shot from that angle at the German tank's less heavily armored flanks or rear—although even the less heavily armored portions of a Panzer or a Tiger were vastly stronger than similar areas on a Sherman. At the same time, the Sherman's radio operator would be on the microphone, frantically calling for Allied planes to join the attack—and praying that the sky was clear enough for them to fly.

In Metz, Vink and his tank crew found an apartment house that the Germans had recently abandoned. It was a fancy, four-story affair that had housed Gestapo and SS officers. The Frenchwoman who operated the building had been delighted to see her military tenants depart. The door to the place was firmly locked, and the woman tried to deny the Americans admittance. When Vink produced his Thompson submachine gun to destroy the lock, the woman reassessed her decision, produced her keys and admitted the crew to the building. Vink and his buddies were astonished at the luxury of the place—elegant furnishings, carpets so thick that most of the men chose them for sleeping. That night, as the weary men of the Sixth Armored slept, church bells pealed throughout Metz. Vink went outside into the falling snow to investigate. He saw the streets filled with French on their way to Midnight Mass, seemingly oblivious to the presence of a war unfolding around them. The following day, after a totally atypical Christmas dinner of turkey, dressing and pies, the Sixth Armored Division resumed its trek to Bastogne.

Immediately outside Metz, as the tanks clanked toward Bastogne, they came under shell fire. They also found themselves the target of bombing and strafing runs by Luftwaffe fighters roaring by immediately overhead. Occasionally, the tanks even found themselves under attack by their own aircraft. Daily, the tankers were supposed to tie across the back of each tank a three-by-six colored vinyl panel to identify them to Allied aircraft as friendly fighting vehicles. Occasionally, however, word would not reach the advance tanks as to which color to display that day, making them fair game for their own tank-killing planes. Luckily, no plane could get sufficiently low in the rough, mountainous country through which the tanks were moving to do much damage.

Three of the five men in Vink's tank were, like him, replacements. They'd been trained to expect to become targets. They performed under fire as the Army expected them to perform—going about their jobs with methodical, fatalistic calm. There was, of course, no other course of action available to them. Their only weapon of defense against air attack was the .50-cal. machine gun atop the tank, which enjoyed a turning radius of 360 degrees and could fire upward. The .30-cal. machine guns, mounted on ball turrets lower on the tank, were

designed to fire at ground targets. Those weapons and the 75
MM cannon were essentially useless against an air attack. As
a result, for all its weight and firepower, the tank was little
more than a huge, slowly moving target with a brightly colored panel over its vulnerable gas tank and only limited ability to defend itself against an enemy swooping down from the
sky.

Consequently, tank convoys tended to hide in the
woods during the day and move only at night, when the
Luftwaffe was essentially blind. Nightly, however, as the tanks
rolled toward Bastogne, a single Luftwaffe hunter would
cruise overhead. The plane emitted a distinctive, ragged
sound. The tankers nicknamed the pilot Bed Check Charlie.
The German pilot would fly slow and low, keeping an eye
peeled for any sort of light—the flare of a match, the glare of a
flashlight on a map. Then he would drop his bomb, never
knowing if the ordinance had done damage. Bed Check
Charlie would then move on with impunity, since any return
fire from the tanks would betray their position and ex-
pose them to a shower of more precise bombing from the night
sky.

Fighting ice and storms across rugged mountains—a
stretch of road referred to by the tankers as Skyline Drive—the
Sixth Armored Division arrived at Bastogne two days after
Christmas. They found the little town surrounded by German
forces and the Fourth Armored Division already in place,
staving off German assaults.

Bastogne had been a bucolic farming village, with
houses attached to barns for warmth, arrayed around a church
in the center of town. Now completely ringed by German
forces, Bastogne was the center of a circle of endless fire, with
German shells sailing in routinely and German infantry constantly probing for weaknesses in the Allied perimeter. When
the Sad Sack pulled in, the snow-covered village was a pile of
bomb rubble. Roofs were missing. Most residents had fled to
surrounding communities or set up residence in the snowy
woods outside the village. Vink and his comrades found one

family living in the sewer—sleeping in bunk beds in a ready-made bomb shelter that was vastly safer than the frozen world above.

The Sad Sack and the other tanks of the Sixth Armored Division were formed into a steel wall around Bastogne, cannons pointing outward toward the fields and forest. Vink's tank was assigned to the end of the line, next to the railroad tracks. The tank crews didn't realize it, but they were about to begin to withstand two four-week sieges—one by German forces determined to stop the allies before they reached the boundary to the Fatherland and the other by the most hellish winter weather imaginable. Snow fell almost daily. Temperatures dropped to well below zero nightly. Tank turrets froze into position in the bitter cold. Ice formed in the cannon barrels and could be removed only by a perilous technique—by pouring gasoline down the barrel and setting it afire, while everybody involved prayed that the entire tank would not burst into flame.

The northern European winter was every bit as bitter a foe as the Wehrmacht. In a torrent of enemy fire, the most common Allied injuries were cold-related. Toes swelled and blackened. Vink quickly found that his feet had swollen so seriously from frostbite that he was unable to get his boots on unless he abandoned his socks. His only relief from the swelling was to leave his tank once an hour during the winter darkness and stand in the snow, barefoot. During the day, when leaving the tank would have been suicidal, the tankers simply suffered with the foot swelling as they waged war from their fighting machines.

The tankers found consolation in the knowledge that if they enjoyed only limited movement in the hip-deep snow, the Germans were in the same fix. Unlike the infantrymen, who were dug into foxholes in the deep snow and frozen mud—foxholes often created with their fingernails—the tankers enjoyed the shelter of their rolling weapons. They slept crumpled up in the tanks. The tons of iron and steel captured all the bone-chilling cold, and the Shermans lacked any internal heat source. The intense cold was as fierce as anything Vink had ever encountered growing up in a snow-belt city on the Hudson where winters were cruel and lengthy.

Meals were haphazard affairs. For the most part, tankers dined on canned food—C-rations. One can might contain ham and eggs. Another might contain hash or franks and beans. For the most part, the food was consumed cold, sometimes even frozen solid. During a lull in fighting, a crew member might escape through the top hatch and place C-rations in pails hung from one of the four manifolds on the rear of the tank. Given enough time, heat from the manifold could produce a hot meal, but the price of that luxury was exposure to enemy fire. If action resumed while the cans were warming they generally were forgotten and ended up exploding in the pail as bombs and shellfire rained down around the tank.

The Army perceived that tankers, unlike the infantry, had unique dietary needs. So, in addition to the C-rations, they also were issued special cases of food called ten-in-one rations. Each case consisted of five days of meals for each crew—powdered milk and lemonade, hard biscuits, cereal and copious quantities of cheese designed to bind up the tankers' bowels and reduce their need to leave the tank to perform bodily functions. The idea was to keep the men in the tank and to keep the tank ready to fight.

The atmosphere inside the tank was distinctly rank. Each man wore the same uniform, including the same long underwear, for week after week. Once, while Vink's tank was briefly pulled out of action to undergo repairs, the Army delivered a unit of portable showers, but the water heaters failed. The grateful tankers nonetheless showered in the icy water, thankful for some way to scrub away the grime, before putting back on their stiff, reeking uniforms and returning to duty.

The tanks maintained their steel circle around Bastogne at night, fending off attacks by both German infantry and armor. They received their orders via runners, to deny the Germans access to those orders via radio interceptions, or after meetings between the tank commanders and brass every morning at the unit command post. During the day, operating on the basis of orders whose larger strategic purpose remained a mystery to them all, the tankers would roll out of Bastogne heading northward, trying to take towns further north to pave the way into Germany. Vink's unit took one town five days in a row—a community only about four miles from their stronghold in Bastogne—but was forced to retreat back out of it every night because of a lack of infantry support to hold that new piece of real estate. The infantry served as the eyes of the tanks, scouting ahead and relaying back information about the strength of enemy resistance, the location of enemy artillery and tanks and the likelihood of air attack. And infantrymen were hard to come by at that juncture in the Battle of the Bulge. Their numbers had been reduced by the initial German assault on Bastogne.

There was, however, no shortage of tanks. Tiny Bastogne was ringed by thousands of them. And the American tankers soon discovered that their 75 MM cannon posed only a negligible threat to the larger, better-made German tanks, especially the immense Tigers. While a direct hit from a Sherman 75 MM cannon needed to strike a Tiger in some small, vulnerable spot, a direct hit from one of the Tiger's 88 MM cannon on a Sherman was likelier than not to set the smaller fighting machine instantly ablaze.

In all, Vink went through five tanks during the Battle of the Bulge. They rolled over mines, were disabled by enemy fire and or simply failed mechanically beyond the capability of the crews to repair them. At that point, the tanks simply were abandoned in the field to be recovered and rebuilt. Sherman tanks in the Battle of the Bulge were large, complex machines subjected to brutal conditions—as were the men who operated them.

For Doug Vink, the most unnerving tank failure took place on New Year's Day 1945. Tank commanders had returned to their crews from the morning meeting at the command post. The Allies were finally breaking out, the commanders told their crews. The crews were to get into their tanks and begin rolling north in force in the direction of the Fatherland. All along the line, men scrambled through hatches into their positions. Tank engines rolled into life, spewing clouds of steamy exhaust into the icy winter air. In the Sad Sack, the driver jammed the vehicle into gear, the tracks began to turn and, just as the tank rolled into motion, Vink and his comrades felt a tremendous force slam into their vehicle. The 88,000-pound tank jumped sideways, as though it had been rammed into by a train.

The crew immediately climbed out of the tank and inspected it. The tank had been struck by a shell from a railway gun—a huge cannon that the Germans moved around on flatbed rail cars that fired 240 MM ordinance. This shell had no doubt been launched from many miles away. The shell was jammed into the sprocket of the track, paralyzing the tank. Luckily, the shell hadn't exploded, as it was designed to do. The men speculated that the shell had been constructed in a slave labor factory and that a worker had sabotaged it, saving all their lives. The tank, however, was now useless. Another had to be brought up for Vink's crew.

"So," he recalled decades later, "we got out, made a bonfire in back of the tank and put our coffee pot on."

Five hours later, a new tank was brought up, and the men of the new Sad Sack scrambled up the road to catch up with their unit. Shortly after the breakout, Vink's regular tank commander, a sergeant, was transferred to another outfit. On the next foray into the German-occupied countryside, Vink found his tank commanded by a young officer—a college boy who'd received his commission after three months of intense training in management and leadership. Such officers were sneeringly referred to by the enlisted men as "90-day wonders." They were not highly regarded by the tank crews they were supposed to lead. This one was immediately nicknamed "Mousy." It was not a term of endearment.

Tanks generally stayed on the roads, which were routinely swept for enemy mines, and avoided open farmland, where mine-sweeping was a far less meticulous process. On this day, however, Mousy ordered the tank off the road and into the fields. He didn't bother to explain his reasoning, and the crew complied with trepidation. In fairly short order, the new Sad Sack struck a mine. The bone-jarring explosion drove the fighting machine several feet into the air. It landed with a clanking thud, one of its tracks broken in half, leaving the Sad Sack paralyzed in a sea of mud about a mile from the safety of Allied lines. The tank's transmission had cracked open. Thirty two gallons of transmission fluid was pouring out into the mud. Heat generated by the explosion had ignited the oil— and, probably, gas from a cracked fuel tank—which was beginning to burn beneath the Sherman. The crew grabbed their small arms and scrambled from the smoking tank before the flames reached the gas tank.

"We looked around for the 90-day wonder," Vink recalled decades later, "and he was gone. We could hear him yelling to us to go back and get our gas masks, and we told him to go to hell."

Mousy had decided to make his way back to the main body of the invading force via the road, which was under constant surveillance by the Germans. That struck Vink as a perilous course of action, and he rejected that escape option. With Mousy no longer on the scene, Vink, as gunner, assumed command. He led his crew into the forest at the edge of the field, hoping to get everybody back to Bastogne through the relative shelter of the woods. Once amid the trees with his crew, Vink counted noses. One man was missing. He could be only one place—back in the burning tank. Vink tore out of the woods and back into the open. As smoke and flames consumed the Sherman, Vink scrambled atop it and back down into the compartment.

The assistant driver, a midwesterner named Lenenbrink, was trapped. The impact of the tank being driven upward by the mine's explosion and then crashing back to earth had spun the tank's turret. The 75 MM cannon rested squarely atop the assistant driver's hatch. Lenenbrink's face was black with soot. Flames and smoke had damaged his eyes. Lenenbrink was blind and worried about staying that way. Using the hand crank, Vink twisted the cannon turret away from the assistant driver's hatch. He then pulled Lenenbrink from the tank and dragged him through the mud of the field to the relative safety of the snowy woods. Then Vink and the other crew members made their way cautiously through the woods to the Allied lines. Lenenbrink was handed over to medical personnel to be evacuated. Vink never heard how he made out.

Doug Vink did, however, cross paths again with Mousy. Ordered into a new tank, Vink found the young officer commanding a detachment of which Vink was a part. Soured by the experience with the mine, Vink was not thrilled to find himself once again subject to Mousy's military judgment. Not many days later, the Sad Sack found itself along with a number of other Shermans sitting high on a hill, essentially atop a cliff, gazing down on a detachment of German soldiers who were, inexplicably, engaging in close order drill.

"So," Vink recalled, "he comes around—the second lieutenant, the 90-day wonder—and he comes over to our tank. . . . He says, 'I want to take two of your men.' I said, 'For what?' He says, 'We're going to snipe.' I said, 'You can't do that. You can't leave these tanks with no people in them.' He said, 'Well, I'm taking them anyway.' He didn't take any people out of my tank, but he went down to another tank, and he took two guys out. He started to shoot. The Germans started to fire back. He got two of the guys wounded. Then a ricochet hit a rock, and he got hit with splinters from the stone. He was rolling around, crying, 'I'm hit! I'm hit! I'm hit!' So, we called the medics and had him taken back. That was the last we saw of him."

Once inside Germany, Vink's crew was firing its cannon continually, launching one 75 MM shell after another at enemy tanks, some as far away as 2,000 yards, others only a few hundred feet in front of the big gun's opening, as infantry behind and in front of the tanks did battle with the enemy's infantry with small arms and mortars. Warfare between tanks was a constant flurry of motion and cannon fire, as Allied tanks tried to draw the Tigers and Panzers into pursuit of one tank while other Shermans would maneuver to the side of the chase and try to hit the Panzer or Tiger from the side or rear. Shermans also delighted in plunging directly into a line of German tanks, firing their 75 MM cannons as they zigged and zagged among enemy fighting machines fearful of firing on the Allies and instead striking one of their own with a missed shot.

Tank gunners were surprisingly accurate at close range. Four in five of Vink's shots connected, although a 75 MM shell striking the armored face of a Panzer or Tiger tended to be a waste of ammunition. The single advantage of Shermans over Panzers or Tigers was the automated turret and cannon. American tankers could swirl the turret, aim and fire in a matter of seconds simply by pushing buttons. German tank turrets and guns had to be hand-cranked. The technical edge generally permitted Shermans to get off the first and, usually, the second shot in most engagements with Tigers or Panzers. After two shots, the Sherman commander would then run like hell before the German commander could get off his own shot in response.

For tanks on either side, accuracy at 2,000 yards was a more complex matter. The tank commander could estimate the distance only visually and adjust the angle of the cannon as he deemed appropriate to loft a shell on a target more than a mile away. Close combat was equally dicey simply because of the sheer, brute power of the machines. On one occasion, Vink saw a Sherman and a Tiger round a corner in a bombed-out village and end up nose-to-nose. The startled gunners fired simultaneously at point-blank range. Each tank was knocked over on its side by the impact of the other's shell.

A tank in battle could exhaust its supply of shells in fairly short order. It would then pull off the battlefield and wait for nightfall, when the Red Ball Express would bring up more ammunition under cover of darkness. The effect of so much firing was to heat up the cannon's barrel. It was later in the battle that another tank from which Vink was fighting failed in that way. Finally, a shell being inserted into the cannon swelled when it came in contact with the hot barrel and could neither be properly loaded nor removed. Vink and his comrades pulled their tank into cover, unable to fight on that day, and watched as the rest of their outfit roared around them, moving steadily forward into the Fatherland.

Engine failure took still another tank. The 500-horsepower engines in Shermans had originally been designed to power aircraft. They were supposed to be air-cooled, but they were encased in heavy metal in compartments where cool air was hard to come by. When they got hot enough, they would seize up, stranding their crews on the battlefield. When that happened, tankers would abandon their fighting machines and try to make their way back to friendly lines to get another tank.

"That's the only way we beat the Germans," Vink said many years later. "It wasn't that we were superior to them, but we had more equipment. We could break down and get another piece of equipment, where they couldn't. . . . They were so far extended that they couldn't get equipment to fight with."

Fighters on the battlefield were isolated from the larger strategy determined by the generals. The Bulge battlefield stretched out over several countries. Nobody in the field knew what was happening elsewhere in the field. Success was measured by a single standard—by ground covered, day in and day out. Allied soldiers knew they were moving forward while the Germans were now moving backward once again. Moreover, they understood why they were winning. Hoofprints in the snow told American tankers that the Germans had been reduced to using horses to move their artillery. Every available drop of gas was going into the Tigers and the Panzers, and the Germans clearly had too little to keep their tanks going much longer. As the Sixth Armored Division rolled steadily northward out of Bastogne, firing their 75 MM cannons relentlessly and rearming and refueling at night, they rolled by countless much deadlier German tanks, sitting useless without gas.

Abandoned by their defeated, despairing crews.

Gun similar to the one that fired on Doug Vink's
tank at the Bastogne breakout
(*Associated Press Photo*)

Infantrymen on the move towards Bastogne

AL COHEN

☆ ☆

Machine gunners worked as a team. They moved about the battlefield on Jeeps except when supporting a specific rifle squad, when all the equipment had to be carried on foot. They would set up and fire their weapon according to orders or as necessitated by incoming enemy fire. The barrel of the .30-cal. water-cooled machine gun was encased in a steel tube to which was linked a container of liquid—water in warm weather, anti-freeze in colder conditions. Throughout the Battle of the Bulge, the water tank was always filled with anti-freeze. Often the only way to melt the ice that tended to freeze the gun's moving parts was to pour anti-freeze on it, or for squad members to urinate on the weapon.

One member of the three-man squad was responsible for carrying ammunition and making certain that it was available at all times. Another squad member carried the tripod on which the gun would rest when set up for action. The third was responsible for the gun itself. When the squad came under fire, the gun could be set up and spewing slugs literally within seconds. That was, in fact, often the squad's only means of self-preservation—setting up the gun in a flash and firing back ferociously across the snowy landscape at whoever was firing on them.

The day after Al Cohen and his buddies learned they were to serve as machine gunners and not as mortar men, during the first week of January 1945, they moved by Jeep to another snow-encrusted village and were attached to a rifle company. The village had recently been wrested from German troops. The squad set up their gun at the village perimeter and spent the night in bed rolls in the snow and ice. The next day they moved out on foot, marching through a landscape of burned-out tanks and other war debris to another village.

By the third day, Cohen was frozen through and getting sick. As the squad trekked through Belgium and crossed into Luxembourg, he found himself coughing and feverish. The squad's medic treated Cohen's illness with a form of high-powered aspirin called APCs. It was a more or less uniform medication, administered liberally to treat ailments as varied as pulmonary infections, muscle aches, fever, and just about any malady short of gunshot wounds and broken bones. The APCs had no discernible effect on Cohen's increasingly serious illness. Finally, the medic led Cohen to a nearby aid station, where he could sit by a stove as he underwent an examination.

"The doctor took my temperature," Cohen recalled. "It was a hundred and one. He said, 'We'll have to send you back to the hospital.' I said I didn't want to go."

You're going, the physician told Cohen, and the unit First Sergeant was brought in to enforce the decision. The sergeant relieved Cohen of his rifle, wrote out some paperwork for him and loaded him on a Jeep. Two hours later, the Jeep deposited Cohen at the bombed-out, two-story building that served as the sector's Allied field hospital. Old mattresses and straw were plugged through the holes in the walls made by artillery shells. Army blankets draped the windows to keep out the cold. Inside, rows of cots were lined up, side by side. The place overflowed with soldiers with respiratory problems. Another doctor took Cohen's temperature, which had risen a full point. You're too bad to stay here, the doctor informed Cohen. He ordered Cohen loaded into an ambulance and transferred to another hospital further back from the lines in Luxembourg. That medical facility turned out to be about 100 cots crammed into a large room in some public building. The placed was jammed with soldiers who, like Cohen, were either on the brink of pneumonia or fully swept up in acute respiratory distress. Cohen spent two days on a cot, receiving medication that induced deep sleep. He would come awake for brief moments, glancing about, taking it all in. The nurses seemed to be on hand every moment. Their shifts finished, they would stay at the hospital to help sick soldiers write letters home. Cohen would drift back to sleep, impressed by their dedication.

"On the third day," Cohen recalled later, "a doctor came around and said, 'How do you feel?' I said, 'Well, I've stopped coughing.' So, he said, 'Okay, tomorrow you go back to your outfit.' A half hour later, they handed me my clothes. I got dressed. There was a Jeep going up to my outfit, so I went back."

Back on the line, Cohen learned that one of his buddies from the trip over had been wounded in the abdomen and shipped back to the States for medical treatment. Then the squad moved out. The squad was always moving out, always moving north.

Into the Dragon's Teeth.

☆ ☆ ☆

Back on the line, Cohen's squad was moving up toward Germany along a road when they encountered some Allied soldiers escorting about a half dozen captured German soldiers to the rear, perhaps even for shipment back to Camp Robinson in Arkansas. The replacement troops studied the prisoners carefully as they passed by. For the first time on the battlefield, they were seeing the enemy up close.

Cohen recalled, "They looked just as scared as we were at times. They looked kind of motley, too—although we didn't look much better to them, I'm sure. We were wet and muddy. So were they."

Attached to a rifle company, the machine gunners moved into a new town to discover intact buildings instead of the rubble they'd encountered in every previous town. They moved into one building, which had been some sort of resort before the shooting started. Beside a window, they set up their gun on a table with a linen tablecloth. They slept inside that night, beneath a solid roof, as the bitter winter wind bounced off the glass windows.

"It was paradise," Cohen recalled.

☆ ☆ ☆

The cold was an immense, all-consuming presence. It sank into the soldiers' bones and stayed there, day and night, as they marched in the snow, fought in the snow, slept in the snow. The Germans wore gray woolen field uniforms. American troops wore the same woolen trousers they would have worn as dress uniforms with their Eisenhower jackets. Over the wool pants, they wore fatigues. Beneath them, they wore long underwear. The three layers of clothing were still inadequate to block the icy wind.

The heavy overshoes they wore atop their combat boots made marching difficult. With the overshoes, each foot felt as though it were cast from lead, but the footwear kept feet dry. Wet feet meant kissing goodbye to your toes. Some men had waterproof boots. If such a man was wounded, his boots were taken off and handed to a comrade before the wounded man was shipped to the rear.

In the hospital, Cohen had watched from his cot as a soldier was brought in on a stretcher, his feet black from trench foot. At one point, the soldier reached for his boots. A nurse stopped him.

"You won't need those again," she said softly.

Soldiers drew lots for canvas field jackets and dry socks brought up by supply sergeants. Cohen got lucky and won a lottery for a pair of waterproof green pants, like those worn by engineers, which kept him dry.

"We got into one town," he recalled, "and I found a rabbit skin vest. So, I took that. I wore that until it started to crawl with bugs. It got lousy."

☆ ☆ ☆

It was daylight. The tanks were moving up. The rifle company and its machine gunners were set up in the town to cover the tanks' advance. A storm of German artillery shells began falling, along with mortar fire. Everybody got low and prayed—except Cohen and the other new guys. They remained standing, shocked into immobility and gazing around at the falling shells, marveling at the explosions, paralyzed by the sudden peril of the situation. The veterans, huddled in the snow, shouted at them angrily to hit the deck. The replacements hit the deck.

"After a while," Cohen said, "you could tell by the sound what was coming in and what was going out. When you're lying there, you find out that you know prayers that you never knew you knew."

☆ ☆ ☆

His name was Hubert J. Tyrell, from Indiana. He was a sergeant, the only veteran left in the machine gun squad, leading green recruits like Al Cohen.

"Right off the bat," Cohen recalled, "he told us, 'The more you think about it—about getting killed or hurt—the worse it's going to be. Just don't think about it. The second thing is, when you dig a hole, and you're an ammo man, when the guys on the guns holler ammo, I don't care how deep you dug that hole, you get up and you get that ammo to them.' He was the type of guy that, when he was with you, nothing could happen to you."

A few months later, Tyrell was awarded a battlefield commission and a Silver Star. In later years, after the war, Cohen kept in touch with him. Tyrell had stayed in the Army.

He was a captain in Korea, where U.S. forces lost 1,000 men a month for 37 months. Cohen received a Christmas card from him during the Korean Conflict. It was the last contact he had with Tyrell.

☆ ☆ ☆

The company was taking a town. As the rifle squads moved forward, Cohen and the other machine gunners set up, firing bursts at the German-held territory. The slugs they fired could travel perhaps a mile. In most actions, the gunners were essentially firing blind, in the general direction of the enemy, putting up a hailstorm of lead that they hoped the Germans would walk into or flee from.

The Germans returned fire as they moved out. Their small arms fire was directed mostly at the advancing American rifle company, but artillery and mortars on the other side of the village were directing ordinance against machine gun emplacements. For machine gunners, enemy mortars were always the big worry. When machine gunners were taken out, it was generally by mortar shrapnel or by shells sailing in from big guns a long way away.

As the shells rained down, the machine gunners fired and ducked, fired and ducked. Some of the machine gun squads hadn't had time to dig their guns into position. They were firing weapons laid out atop the snow. Occasionally, as mortar and artillery fire began zeroing in, indicating that the big guns might be operating under the instructions of a German forward observer with a radio, the crews would grab their gear and change position, hoping to get out of the observer's line of sight. If they were lucky, they would find a hole originally dug by German machine gunners. They would drag the German corpses out of the hole and leave them in the snow and take over the position that had been dug by the dead men. They would mount the .30-cal. on its tripod and set up the ammo box. Then they would fire and duck, fire and duck.

And fire and duck some more.

☆ ☆ ☆

It was a day when the weather was warming. Cohen and his squad were on the outskirts of a town. They opened K-rations and began to eat. A breeze ruffled the snow near their foxhole. Cohen glanced over and watched as the wind swirled the snow off the face of a dead German soldier. He kept on eating and watching as the breeze freshened and more of the snow at that spot was blown away. When the face of a dead American soldier appeared in the snow, Al Cohen stopped eating.

☆ ☆ ☆

After three weeks of combat, Cohen and his unit went through the Dragon's Teeth in February. They entered Germany under fire. The Germans had fought ferociously ever since being pushed out of Bastogne. Now, low on gas and worn down, the German army had backed into the Fatherland as the Russians closed on them from the east and as the Allies were moving in on them from the snowfields of northern France, and they were fighting hard at the border. Once Cohen's group got through the pyramid-shaped concrete obstacles, they ended up staying there for several days, as the last vestiges of German resistance at the Dragon's Teeth were eliminated.

The engineering corps had paved the way. Pathways had been blown through the barriers, and the Shermans had poured in followed by infantry. Pillboxes that were part of the fortifications were bombarded by 75 MM shellfire from the tanks. When that had proved ineffective in destroying the pillboxes, mobile 155 MM cannon were moved up to finish the job. Once through the Dragon's Teeth, Cohen and his squad set up their machine gun near an abandoned farmhouse and used it to command the rolling hills of the German landscape. They fired out at the pillboxes, keeping the German defenders trapped inside, while the 155s reduced the emplacements to rubble.

"There was one pillbox, Cohen recalled many years later. "I think that every GI who went through the Dragon's Teeth went through this one pillbox to see what it was like inside. There was one German lying on a canvas slab—a bunk. He was hanging half on, half off, his eyes wide open. And wherever you walked in that pillbox, his eyes would seem to follow you. It was creepy."

As a lack of gas rendered their ferocious tanks useless, and as Allied soldiers and tanks poured through pathways blasted through the Dragon's Teeth into the Fatherland, the Germans continued to fight hard. Cohen's outfit followed behind the tanks, moving toward Bavaria and Czechoslovakia into heavily shelled villages to clean out pockets of German soldiers and digging through the woods for stragglers or suicide rear guard troops. All along, Allied troops had been opposed not only by the regular German army, the Wehrmacht, but also by Hitler's special Nazi Party troops, the Schutzstaffel, known as the SS, headed by Hitler deputy Heinrich Himmler. The SS not only ran the concentration camps dedicated to the extermination of Jews, they operated outside the jurisdiction of the Wehrmacht commanders and constituted a separate German army. Now, as the Allies marched on the soil of the Fatherland, they found themselves fighting members of a third army—Germany's home guard. This was composed of men in their 60s who'd first tasted blood in the trenches of World War I.

And kids. Inside the Fatherland, the fuzzy-cheeked teenagers of the Hitler Youth were handed guns and sent out into the field to fight and die for the Third Reich.

"They were just as tough as the others," Cohen recalled. "We had our guns set up in this one village, and they brought up an anti-tank gun and put it near us. We had a building that would permit us to get out of the weather. We came out of that building at that point, and some lieutenant had a kid of about 14 years old. The kid was crying.

"We asked the lieutenant what was going on. He said that two of these kids had come up to him and clicked their heels and went, 'Heil Hitler!' One of them wanted to die for the Fuhrer, so the lieutenant obliged him. Then the other kid decided that he didn't want to die for the Fuhrer after all. So, the lieutenant took this kid and put him over his knee and paddled his rear. Then they sent the kid back to the PW cage.

"That's what you got. Some of them decided they didn't want to die. Some of them were real little bastards."

☆ ☆ ☆

The rifle company was taking a German town at the bottom of a high hill. Cohen and his fellow machine gunners were in Jeeps crawling up one side of the hill, with only a limited view of what was occurring below the summit, down on the other side, where the fighting was occurring. Their orders were to set up their gun atop the hill and provide covering fire for the riflemen. Their vantage point would give them a view of most of the town and the open land beyond, where the Germans would flee as they were pushed backward, backward, steadily backward toward Berlin.

"We're standing there having a cigarette," Cohen recalled. "By that time, we were going through four or five towns in one day with not much resistance. I've got the machine gun resting on my foot. And the first gunner has the tripod on his back, and we're bullshitting. And all of a sudden we look down, and the ground is popping up about two inches from our feet—pop, pop, pop—no sound, but you could see the dirt flying."

They were being fired on. Machine gun slugs were flying in from some distant location where somebody they couldn't see had seen them and was bent on killing them. It was the scariest sort of fire—the kind they couldn't hear, and it was always the one you didn't hear that got you.

Cohen said many years later, "I think we held the record that morning for setting up that gun and getting it firing. Over on the other side of town, we saw a line of people. We couldn't tell what they were, but we saw the long over-coats, like the Germans wore, and we figured that was them, so we started firing at them. They must have been a mile, a mile-and-a-half away."

Once they'd quenched the enemy fire, the machine gun squad packed up and moved down the hill into the town. Moving along a street, with gunfire sounding around a corner, they came upon a commercial building. Miraculously, its gigantic plate glass window was still intact. They stopped and gazed at the thing, amazed to see this window in one piece after all the intense shelling this German town had endured. They realized that they were looking at the village bank.

"Then this bazooka man comes up the street," Cohen recalled. "He says, 'What are you guys looking at?' We said, 'This window on the bank.' He says, 'Get out of the way.' He takes the bazooka, and he fires one round through the window. You don't hear a sound, but you see money floating out the window. Then you hear the explosion."

After the war, Cohen learned that all the German money in the bank could have been redeemed and exchanged for American greenbacks. At the time, though, the machine gun squad figured that the bills floating in the street could be put to immediate and practical use.

As toilet paper.

Allied soldiers crossing the Rhine
(*Associated Press Photo*)

Doug Vink (at left) with munitions

DOUG VINK

☆ ☆

One of the harsh realities of tank warfare was the need for tanks to communicate with one another and with commanders behind the lines via radio. Each member of a tank crew wore a small, leather helmet with built-in earphones. Tankers knew that any electronic communication could be, and probably was, monitored by the Germans. That meant that the location of Allied tanks was seldom a mystery to the enemy. It meant that artillery spotters always knew where to find them. Consequently, tankers never knew when to expect an attack—never knew when shells might begin falling on them from afar. The 88 MM cannons used by the Germans had a greater range than the Sherman 75 MM cannons. Tankers also never knew when strafing Luftwaffe fighters packing tank-killing bombs might swoop down from the clouds.

"The Germans seemed to know where everybody was all the time," Vink recalled six decades later. "We sat one time by the Our River. The Germans had our tank sighted in. My commander was a Sergeant Hicks. He was from the South. Nice guy, but strict; you had to be . . . the Germans fired a shell across the river from us, and it hit just in front of us. So, the commander says to the driver, 'Back up.' So we back up about eight feet. The next shell hit right where we'd been before we moved. We then went back about six or seven times, and every time a new shell hit where we had been. So, finally, we smartened up, and the commander said, 'Pull ahead, all the way up to the river.' Well, we must have gotten out of sight of the spotter because the next shell hit where we'd been before, and we got no more after that. We were finally out of his line of sight."

The Sad Sack's crew could see no Germans across the river, no target on which they could return fire. The German guns probably were back beyond the forest, out of sight. The spotter, like most German troops, probably was clad in white, the better to hide himself in the snow. American infantrymen did not wear snow camouflage. For a tanker, there was no place to hide, anyway. Crews couldn't dig foxholes for their tanks. Moving into stands of trees was an option frequently taken, but such a move meant that the tank's cannon turret would lose its ability to swivel 360 degrees to repel a sudden enemy attack. So, when they used their radios, tankers became vulnerable, but they also understood that there existed a compelling need to maintain communication, to stay in touch with fellow fighting machines, despite the inherent dangers of radio transmission.

One reason for the need to use radios was the topography surrounding Bastogne. That portion of Belgium was a collection of rolling, hilly farm fields separated by thick stands of tall pine trees. Visibility was limited by geology and geography. Tankers never knew what might lie over the next hill.

Doug Vink served in C Company—radio code name Charlie Company—consisting of about 200 men and 18 tanks. Over the radio, the company commander was designated Charlie One. Other, lower-level commanders—platoon leaders or platoon sergeants, each commanding about 50 men— were Charlie Two and Charlie three, and so on. Through such designations, and with the aid of maps, tank commanders were able to ascertain where they were, where their comrades were and where they were likely to happen upon German tanks or defensive emplacements. As with all wartime operations, however, the theory generally proved more reliable than the reality. Once the firing began, everyone on the battlefield on either side was engaged mainly in a mad scramble for survival—an outcome that usually could be assured only by a victory, by killing the enemy.

For tankers in the Battle of the Bulge, sleep was little more than a rumor even when the tank was motionless and its engine silent. They slept only at brief intervals, and a crew member stood in the turret every second, head protruding from the hatch opening, exposed and listening and watching and opening fire on anything that looked even remotely suspicious.

"You stand in that turret long enough at night," Vink later recalled, "and what was a bush during the day starts to move on you, so you shoot at it. There was no night vision equipment, and after a while in the turret your eyes could start to play tricks on you."

The worst time, the most perilous period, was between 4 and 7 AM. It was dark. Crews slept fitfully in their tanks, their senses dulled by physical and mental exhaustion coupled with a few hours of inactivity. A guard on duty in the turret was especially vulnerable during that time period to spotting movement where there was none. By the same token, if there really was movement, it was most likely to occur during those dangerous hours just before dawn, and everybody knew it. Generally, strands of wire rigged with flares and grenades were arrayed around the sleeping tank crews to fend off invaders. Infantrymen on both sides understood: Step on the wire in the darkness, and that action could pull out the pin of a grenade and send you to your death in an explosion that split the silence of the night. Accidentally ignite a flare on the wire, and suddenly you were a vividly illuminated target for some tank's machine guns. The wire wasn't always in place, though, especially if the tanks were positioned for the night ahead of the main lines.

Early on one such morning, with the Sad Sack and several other tanks having spent the night backed into a stand of woods outside Bastogne without the benefit of trip-wire protection, Vink had relieved the tank commander on guard duty. Standing in the turret, peering out into the pre-dawn darkness,

Vink became certain that he was seeing movement in the snow. What Vink had spotted was a smallish brown shape moving through the shadowy whiteness in front of the tank. A rabbit, perhaps? From the turret, he gazed more intently. There was movement there; he definitely was seeing movement.

After a few moments of intense study, Vink came to realize that the brown shape was the moving butt of a German Mauser rifle. White-clad German troops were crawling in on the sleeping tanks to stage a killing assault just before the sun rose. After alerting his commander, Vink popped back up in the turret to unload on the Germans with his .30-cal. machine gun. Other guards in other tanks reacted to the sound of machine gun fire by loosing their own. For perhaps a minute, machine gun fire tore into German invaders only a few feet from the Sad Sack. None of the invading Germans survived. As the machine gun fire died down, and as day's light intensified, the tank crews gazed out on several dozen Wehrmacht soldiers lying motionless in the bloodstained snow in front of the stand of tall pine trees.

Such commonplace bursts of machine gun fire, both at legitimate dangers and at shadows, tended to produce rocky sleeping sessions for tank crew members. When quiet sleep time was available, the crews dozed in the tank or, if they could find a house with even a small patch of roof remaining, would collapse inside the structure wrapped up in sleeping bags— commonly referred to by tankers and infantrymen alike as "fart sacks." At one point in the ordeal, Vink and his buddies found such a house, but the stairs leading inside had been destroyed. They managed to gain access to the building only by stacking up the frozen corpses of dead German soldiers to create a set of steps.

Inside the tank, the only light came from a "Little Joe"— a gas-powered electrical generator that plugged into the vehicle just behind the turret, keeping the tank's batteries charged and providing limited illumination inside the compartment. When the Little Joe was not in operation, tankers depended on flashlights. Because of the darkness and irregular sleeping hours, days tended to blend into one another with no sharp lines of demarcation between them. As a result, most of Doug Vink's memories of that time existed nearly 60 years later as isolated incidents rather than as an orderly sequence of events.

When the Sixth Armored Division pulled into Bastogne, Vink's most vivid impression of the town was the extent of the devastation that had been visited upon it. The Sad Sack took up a position about a mile and a half out of town, with a French armored outfit to its right. Shortly thereafter, the French were relieved by an American armored division, and the Sad Sack found itself pulled off the line as well. Vink's crew rolled back into Bastogne, searching for a place to park so they could sleep. The tank was always parked with its gun pointing out into the countryside beyond the bombed-out village, so it could be moved into action in a hurry if necessary. That night, however, German shelling of Bastogne and on the line of Allied tanks surrounding the village intensified, so the rest period the Sad Sack's crew had anticipated was cut short. They were sent back out on the line to hold off any German attack that might follow the bombardment. As the Sad Sack settled into its position in the line, infantry moved into the field in front of the line to feel around, to see if German infantry was indeed moving in under the bombardment.

The infantry owned the night. In darkness, tanks were limited by poor visibility and by the immense noise they made. In no way was a Sherman tank a stealthy piece of combat equipment. Despite their fighting vehicle's essential ineffectiveness in darkness, however, tank crews were expected to stay inside the Sherman and protect it. As a result, tankers spent long hours together in their darkened tank compartments, getting to know one another. For most of these young men who'd come of age in Depression-era America, when the huge country's distinct regions were isolated from one another, the war represented their first extended contact with people whose backgrounds were not identical to their own.

"We had a great crew," Vink recalled many decades later. "The driver was from down in Tennessee or some such

area.   Like I was from New York, another kid was from
Pennsylvania. The sergeant was from the Smoky Mountains or
someplace. He was a real guy, a real southerner. The other kid,
he was from out in the Midwest someplace. . . . At night, you
would kibitz back and forth. There was really nothing to talk
about. You don't know anything that's going on. You don't
know the news or anything else. By the time you get the news,
it's a week old. No sense talking about it. So, all we talked
about were the girls back home, about waiting to get back
home, about getting the hell out of this cold."

For Doug Vink and the other tankers, war was long
hours of tedium punctuated by spurts of breathtaking action.
They were fired on daily. After a while, even being under
enemy fire grew tedious.

"It got boring after a while," Vink recalled. "It was the
same thing every day. If somebody fires at you every day and
he doesn't hit you, you're just waiting and asking yourself,
'When the hell is he going to get me?'"

Any break in the routine, therefore, was a welcome
occasion for diversion—like the day a British fighter plane was
shot down in sight of Vink's tank.

"He'd crashed during the day," Vink recalled, "out
behind German lines. We knew where he'd gone down. He
went and hid in the woods for the rest of the day. That night—
and, of course, he didn't know the password or anything else—
he comes walking in right in front of our tank. We got talking
with him after the infantry identified him. Here's a guy with a
silk scarf on, a light jacket and loafers walking in through
waist-deep snow. We played dumb. We said, 'What the hell
are you doing out here?' And he said, 'I'm trying to get back to
England.' I said, 'Well, we're trying to get back to the States.'"

Without knowledge of the day's password, the fighter
pilot knew he was lucky to have avoided the same flurry of
gunfire that had resulted in the quick and bloody deaths of the
white-clad German troops. A typical password would be
"Abraham," and the countersign would be "Lincoln." The
password and countersign would be passed along to tank

crews after the morning commanders' meeting at the command post. Tanks in the field, however, often did not receive word of the password change. Luckily, Sherman tanks, like American aircraft, emitted distinctive sounds that clearly distinguished them from German weaponry.

"You were always seeing somebody walking in," Vink recalled many years later. "Patrols would get lost during the night, and then they'd come into your area. . . . You'd be picking up a lot of civilians. And you'd be wondering what the hell you would do with them? Were they really civilians or were they Germans?"

Most contact with the civilians who weren't always civilians took place during the day as the tanks patrolled the snowy ground outside Bastogne.

"You'd be out in the field," Vink said, "and all of a sudden there were people walking out of the woods. They'd be living out there, driven out of their homes. You didn't know who they were. You didn't know whether to shoot them, to treat them as civilians. The way the Germans were, you could never tell. They would capture your uniforms, which was strictly against the war code, and they would wear them and come in at you—infiltrate your lines in your uniforms. You never knew day to day who it was."

The Allied forces were especially sensitive to the danger of German soldiers in civilian clothing or in American uniforms after that incident early in the Battle of the Bulge in which Peiper's English-speaking German soldiers in American uniforms and piloting American Jeeps had slaughtered unsuspecting U.S. troops.

"When we picked up people dressed as civilians," Vink said, "none of us could speak their language. They'd come out and communicate with hand gestures. If there was infantry around, we'd have them take them back to the command post. If there wasn't any infantry, we'd try to get them back ourselves. Usually, the guy assigned to do that was the poor assistant driver, if we could spare him. But a lot of them ended up shot, especially if they came out in front of you, where there was supposed to be only Germans. . . . I know of different times we'd pick up people, and if we had the infantry with us we'd tell them to take them back. And it would be such a distance that maybe they'd get back in the woods a little bit, and you'd hear some gunfire, and all of a sudden the infantry guy is back, and you'd know that they didn't make it to the command post. It was just one of those unfortunate things."

When conversation petered out in the tank at night, as it often did, there was always the radio. Tank radios came with a wide range of frequencies. With the volume turned down low to keep the tank inconspicuous during the nighttime hours, tankers would tune into news broadcasts, listening through the earphones in their leather helmets for any information that might affect their units or them. They also tuned in regularly to Axis Sally, the Germans' European version of Tokyo Rose. Her job was to lure Allied soldiers to her broadcasts with popular music and then feed them defeatist propaganda and urge them to surrender. You can't win, Axis Sally kept telling the Allied soldiers freezing in the snow; you can never defeat the German soldier.

"Axis Sally had a gorgeous sounding voice," Vink recalled. "She could make you feel like you wanted to get out of that tank and go home. . . . She played all the top music—all the top stuff from the Hit Parade. You'd swear you were home listening to it."

When it came to information rather than music, however, Axis Sally made less of a hit with Allied troops.

Vink recalled, "One time we had fought through Nancy, France. We got way up north of there, and we got orders to move back to Nancy. We had to replace our engines and re-do our tracks and get the whole tank done over. Before we moved, they told us to take all our insignias off, all our patches off, all our stripes and paint the tanks so that no numbers were on them and no identifying marks. And we went back to Nancy. Well, that night, we heard Axis Sally's broadcast, and she was saying that the Sixth Armored Division had been annihilated during the day and that we no longer existed—that the

German army had beaten the whole division. So, we stayed there maybe a week or two and got all our work done. And then we got all new patches and all new stripes, and we got back into action, and the next thing we knew she was saying on the air was that we were a whole new outfit, that the old Sixth Armored was gone and that we were all new guys."

For most of the time the Shermans encircled Bastogne, the skies were gray and ominous. On the day the breakout was ordered, however, the sun broke through the clouds to present the snow as a shimmering, glittering blanket of white. Vink's crew was late getting underway, thanks to the dud shell from the railway gun that disabled their tank as they set out. Hours later, though, in a new tank, Vink's crew finally was rolling through the sun-splashed winter landscape.

"It was a beautiful morning," Vink recalled, "a typical winter morning on which you'd love to be home, looking out at the woods. It was really something to look out through the periscope and see all those tanks, all that equipment, moving at one time. Of course we ran into resistance, which we seemed to break down pretty easily. . . . My company headed out for a place called Michamps. . . . Then we spotted four German tanks coming in toward Michamps and a town called Bourcy. The 11th Armored Division was supposed to be on our right side at that time, but when we looked out we found that they were gone. They'd taken another route and gone down to another outfit without us knowing it."

Charlie Company was undeterred. All 18 tanks continued rolling toward Michamps. They were moving abreast in a skirmish line, side by side, with each tank about 25 feet from the next. Shermans could reach 26 miles per hour, but these fighting machines were moving at about one-third speed as their crews watched the opposition form up before them. The German tanks were about a half mile away, moving toward Michamps. The Sherman crews knew they were well within range of the guns of the German tanks' 88 MM cannons. They also knew that their 75 MM cannons were virtually useless against the frontal armor of the German tanks at that range.

"What complicated things for them," Vink said, "was that there was a little bit of woods between them and us, and they couldn't fire through the trees at us because they'd be hitting tree trunks instead of us. Also, whether they saw us and knew that we were there I never knew. . . . So, what we did was call up the TDs."

The TD, or tank destroyer, was a rolling artillery platform that moved more quickly than a tank and sported a 105 MM Howitzer. It was an open vehicle without a turret, but it carried firepower vastly more potent against the Panzers and Tigers than the Shermans' 75 MM popguns. The two available TDs rolled quickly into position and quickly destroyed all four German tanks at the half-mile range.

Charlie Company's Shermans rolled through Michamps as the crews peered out at the burning German tanks. They kept on moving. Soon they were joined by an infantry company and five more tanks. They weren't sure precisely where they were going, when they would get there or what they might encounter on the way. The important thing was that the tanks were on the move, and the crews knew that the Red Ball Express was coming up behind them to feed their tanks in the coming darkness so they could resume their trek the following morning. The Sixth Armored was grinding ahead, its steel tracks digging into the snow and clanking through it, relentlessly rolling toward the Dragon's Teeth. And, beyond them, into Germany, into the Fatherland, toward Berlin.

"With Patton," Vink recalled, "you didn't stop. If you had gas, you kept moving. . . . The feeling was, 'Well, we accomplished that, and now we're on the move and Lord knows what'll be coming tomorrow.' That's what you did. You took it as it came."

Guns surrendered to American forces by
defeated German troops
(*Associated Press Photo*)

German soldiers killed during the Battle of the Bulge
(*Associated Press Photo*)

THE BULGE

☆ ☆

Hitler's *Wacht am Rhine* strategy called for Dietrich's Sixth Panzer Army and Manteuffel's Fifth Panzer Army to reach the Meuse River in four days. Because of isolated pockets of American resistance and the speed with which Allied fighting forces reacted to the intrusion, that goal was not achieved.

In the southern sector, the German Seventh Army had been held to a virtual standstill, unable to make any significant progress toward Luxembourg or to cover the flank of the Fifth Panzer Army. Hitler's plan to quickly overwhelm the opposition was foundering. Six Allied divisions had delayed 20 German divisions, and Allied reinforcements were pouring into the sprawling battlefield. Hitler, however, had not committed his Sixth Army's II SS Panzer Division. Moreover, he was holding additional divisions and armor in reserve.

In the north, the Second Battalion of the U.S. Army's 82nd Airborne Division had been ordered to head off Peiper and his Sixth Army I SS Panzer Division. The Second Battalion reached Trois-Ponts in time to set up defenses. Then—with no tanks, no tank destroyers and no large artillery—they fought off Peiper's armor. Utilizing hit and run tactics and using small caliber antitank guns and a half dozen bazookas, they forced the German commander to turn north in search of a new bridge to cross. The German spearhead was low on fuel and ammunition as Peiper's quest for a passage across the river near Trois-Pont literally and figuratively ran out of gas. He ended up setting fire to his equipment and walking back to the Siegfried Line.

On December 20th, Eisenhower was forced to make a necessary, though unpopular, decision about command. Bradley's 12th Army had been split north and south of the Bulge. Because the Germans had severed telephone lines, Bradley was unable to maintain communications with his commanders from his Luxembourg headquarters. Eisenhower decided to give British Field Marshal Montgomery's 21st Army Group control of the ground troops in the First and Ninth Army in the northern shoulder of the Bulge, roughly five miles south of St. Vith, and all points north. Montgomery was elated. American generals were furious at the decision. "Monty," still smarting from not being named Supreme Commander in Europe and spurred by complaints from his commanders that they had become secondary participants in the conflict, portrayed himself as the savior of the befuddled Americans—with all their men, machines and equipment. While American commanders wanted to mount an offensive, Montgomery argued for maintaining a defensive posture until all the enemy reserves had been committed and then—once in the open—destroyed. Ike agreed in part to the British strategy and approved a defensive posture in the northern Ardennes while maintaining a corps-sized reserve for a counterattack when the time was right.

While plans were being made to shore up the north, Patton's Third Army was speeding to the aid of the 101st Airborne and other mixed units under siege in and around Bastogne. By now, word had spread around the world of this little town and its heroic defense by a small group of Americans facing overwhelming odds. Maps of the offensive appearing in newspapers showed Bastogne in the center of the Bulge, completely surrounded by German troops, cut off, and alone. The situation was becoming desperate, as the 101st was low on supplies and ammunition.

Near St. Vith, Montgomery issued orders for the

Seventh and Ninth Armored Divisions, as well as the 106th and 28th Divisions, to pull out before they became encircled and trapped by the enemy. Those units had been under constant attack by the advancing Germans. Their ammunition and fuel were in short supply, and Hitler had now committed his II SS Panzer Division under Dietrich to the battle. Mud had threatened to trap most of the Allied defenders before their retreat, but dipping temperatures turned the mushy ground hard enough to allow 100 tanks and two regiments of troops to escape and fold in with the 82nd Airborne front.

On December 22th, Manteuffel ordered much of the Fifth Panzer Army to bypass Bastogne and speed toward the Meuse, leaving the 26th Volksgrenadier Division and XLVII Panzer Artillery to finish off the American holdouts. The German commander left in charge of taking Bastogne sent a message to Brigadier General Anthony McAuliffe demanding his surrender. McAuliffe's one-word reply, "Nuts," became part of military lore. The answer confounded the Germans, and the American defense continued to hold.

The cold front that passed over northern Europe on December 23rd cleared the skies and allowed the air force to join the battle. To his chagrin, Hitler found inclement weather an unreliable ally. Allied planes dropped much-needed supplies to the Bastogne defenders. Allied fighters attacked German troops on roads throughout the Ardennes. Allied bombers flew missions to cripple German supply lines. During the first 10 days of the clash, Allied pilots flew an average of 3,000 sorties a day and dropped more than 31,000 tons of bombs.

The effect was devastating to the Germans, who'd already been slowed by tough terrain and fuel shortages. The Allied air strikes halted the German offensive all along the front. At the tip of the Bulge, the second Panzer Division had run out of gas. The U.S. sent armor and heavy air support to encircle and destroy the force only five miles from the Meuse River. By December 28th, Hitler's drive for Antwerp had been bombed to a halt. Epic ground battles at Baraque de Fraiture,

Manhay, Hotton, Marche-were, St. Vith and Bastogne would forever distinguish American troops for their grit, determination and bravery.

With the death of the western offensive inevitable, Hitler had decided a week earlier to launch a new offensive southeast of the Ardennes in the Alsace region. Operation *Nordwind* (Northwind) would be one of several separate offensives from January 1st to 25th designed to take advantage of Patton's Third Army deployment in the Ardennes. This left only the badly stretched Sixth Army Group to protect the area. *Nordwind* would be Hitler's last offensive gasp. The objective was to capture routes on the way to Strasbourg by attacking through the Vosges Mountains, effectively splitting the Seventh Army and trapping the VI Corps in northeastern France. If successful, the result would be not only the capture of Strasbourg but the weakening of the Allied front in the Ardennes by forcing Allied command to send troops to bolster those being overrun in the Alsace.

The Sixth Army Group was assigned to the southern region under Lt. General Jacob Devers. The Sixth was designated guardian of the southern flank in support of Montgomery's 21st Army Group and Bradley's 12th Army Group, which were chosen by Eisenhower to lead the charge into Germany, when it came. By virtue of its secondary role, the Sixth Army Group was the lowest on the priority list when it came to supply, logistics and personnel. The front along the Rhine in the Alsace region was very much reminiscent of the thinly guarded American salient in the Ardennes prior to the German counteroffensive. The coldest winter in 30 years was accounting for the majority of the casualties through frostbite, trench foot and respiratory aliments. The only difference was that this attack would be no surprise. Allied intelligence, studying intercepted German messages in a program designated Ultra, had deciphered a German transmission and alerted Allied command to Hitler's planned New Year's Eve offensive.

Since D-Day, the Allies had suffered a critical shortage of infantry riflemen—troops who fight in front of light artillery.

When compared to the overall size of the army, infantrymen represented a relatively small group, but they did most of the front line fighting and sustained 90 per cent of the casualties. The battles in the Ardennes and Alsace would be decided almost entirely by the resolve and bravery of the foot soldiers who would absorb virtually all the casualties. During November, the Seventh Army, a part of the Sixth Army Group, had received nine full regiments of ill-trained infantry replacements. These troops originally had been assigned to rear duty only. They were code named Task Forces Linden, Herren and Harris. With a German offensive looming, however, these green troops were sent to front-line defensive positions.

Also during November, the U.S. Seventh Army and the French First Army, each a Sixth Army Group unit, had been able to gain territory on the Alsace plains by breaking through fortified German positions and capturing key passes through the Vosges Mountains. On November 23rd, the French Second Armored Division liberated Strasbourg from the enemy. With the attack in the Ardennes in full swing by late December, a 126-mile front in Alsace that originally had been guarded by only six divisions had been bolstered by the deployment of the new task forces. Unfortunately, Devers' thin defenses would be further stretched when 600 troops from each of the task forces were ordered to the Bulge as infantry replacements.

On December 26th, with word of an enemy attack in the region verified, Eisenhower ordered Devers to withdraw from the Rhine to more easily defensible positions in the mountains. Dever was to relinquish the Alsace plains and, more important, Strasbourg. This became a political hot potato known as the "Strasbourg Incident." French General Charles de Gaulle feared German reprisal against French citizens of the town. With support from Devers, de Gaulle argued successfully against abandoning previously captured areas.

As Ultra had predicted, the Germans attacked on January 1st, south of Bitche. They were bent on capturing passes through the lower Voges Mountains. Over the next several weeks, fierce battles ensued for the icy roads that would allow Hitler's troops to penetrate the salient. In the end, the Germans made no significant gains from Operation *Nordwind* nor from their other hastily launched offensives in the southern region. American and French troops countered and blocked their attempts to achieve control of major roadways. As these encounters played out, the German offensive in the Bulge was dying. Allied troops were driving Hitler's forces back toward the Siegfried Line.

Throughout most of January, monumental head-to-head confrontations would result in high casualties for both armies in the Ardennes and Alsace. Hitler gave up captured territory only grudgingly, and his propensity for withholding approval for withdrawal until the last possible moment cost thousands of lives on each side. Plagued by the worsening weather, Allied forces took nearly three weeks after halting *Wacht am Rhine* before driving the enemy back into Germany. The final tally of casualties in the Ardennes would total over 80,000 for the Allies, with 19,000 killed. As many as 100,000 Germans were killed or wounded. In the Alsace region, the Seventh Army reported another 11,000 casualties with German losses estimated at 23,000. Allied soldiers succumbing to sickness and cold injuries accounted for 17,000 hospitalized during both campaigns.

The most important battle in world history had ended. Its outcome had been determined not by brilliant generalship or by the quality of military hardware. In the end, the Allies had won because the bitter winter weather had not been quite bad enough to ground their planes, because the Germans had run short of gas and because youthful, inexperienced GI's shivering in the snow had fought with such astounding gallantry and resolve.

Hitler had expended much of his manpower, equipment and supplies in these two offensives—resources that he otherwise would have had available to defend the Fatherland and, perhaps, to have permitted him to hunker down behind the Dragon's Teeth and negotiate an armistice. The physical toll of the battle was nothing when compared to damage to the morale of German soldiers and civilians. While more fighting lay ahead, the road to Berlin was essentially open to the Allies. In fewer than two months the invasion into Germany would be complete. Americans and British would surround the city as they waited for the Russians to arrive and enter on April 23rd. A week later, Adolf Hitler would commit suicide in his bunker deep beneath the bombed-out wreckage of Berlin.

On May 7, 1945, as spring washed over northern Europe, Germany would offer the Allies its unconditional surrender.

Infantrymen in the snowy woods of
Belgium's Ardennes Forest
(*Associated Press Photo*)

AL COHEN

☆ ☆

The Germans had been building weaponry since 1934, and they'd built it deftly. Their tanks were better than anything the Allies had. Their 88 MM artillery weapon was used both as a field piece and as the cannon on their tanks, simplifying the problem of supplying shells to warriors on the battlefield. The Luger, the standard German pistol, was a vastly better weapon than the American .45-cal. automatic—lighter, better balanced and, if less powerful, more accurate at greater range. GI's took possession of them from enemy soldiers at every opportunity. The Browning .30-cal. machine gun that Al Cohen and his buddies operated had been designed in 1917. The German machine guns were newer and meaner.

It was the German mines, however, that killed without warning, that unnerved Allied riflemen. They were saucer-shaped, packed with ball bearings and other shrapnel and exploded about waist level on their victims—leaping into the air after being tripped. Cohen and other infantrymen had been taught in basic training how to crawl forward on their hands and knees while probing with bayonets into the dirt in front of them. In the field, though, they learned that in areas they could expect to be mined they were wise to follow behind engineering outfits. The engineers sought out mines with metal detectors and, occasionally, could clear a mine field with huge rolling bulldozers fitted in the front with giant steel wheels or rolling tillers and steel shields—gear designed to set off the mines and block the operator from shrapnel. Snow was an ideal venue for mines. They could be planted more easily and quickly in snow than in dirt, and their was no shortage of snow in northern Europe during the winter of 1944-1945.

The Germans also displayed a distressing affection for booby traps. One of their favorite tricks was to plant explosives along the bottoms of toilet seats in towns and villages they abandoned before the relentless Allied advance. GI's who'd lived for weeks in the snow could be too eager for the luxury of a sojourn on a real toilet. Veterans warned the newer men—check for booby traps; sit down too quickly and you can end up plastered across the bathroom ceiling.

Once through the Dragon's Teeth and moving behind the tanks, Cohen's platoon came upon a building about 30 feet long. They explored it with care. Everybody wanted to get inside, out of the wind. The floor was carpeted with sawdust. In the middle of the building, they came across a German helmet on the floor. The sergeant in charge ordered his men to stay away from it. Instead, standing outside, just beyond the doorway, he lassoed the helmet with a length of rope and dragged it outside. Everybody expected an explosion to erupt the moment the helmet was moved, but none came. Despite the bitter wind and despite the fact that the helmet hadn't been booby trapped after all, the infantrymen chose to bypass the building. They didn't like the looks of the place. Somewhere inside, they were sure, something was rigged to blow up, and they wanted no part of it.

☆ ☆ ☆

In late February, the deep snow began melting and fading into mud. The campaign in Germany dragged on. Up near Frankfurt, what would have been snow only a few weeks earlier now fell as rain. Spring was in the air, wet and bone-chilling. Now Cohen and his machine gun squad qualified as veterans, eyed respectfully by wide-eyed new replacements. As they moved through a town, they and some other men found a house in which to sleep. Miraculously, the building had been untouched by the violence of war, although its inhabitants were nowhere to be found.

"One day," Cohen recalled, "I was sitting on the floor cleaning my rifle, and one of the fellows was reading *Stars and Stripes*. He was one of the older guys—twenty-three or twenty-four. At that time, I carried a carbine. I was putting the bolt in, and he was reading the paper, and he suddenly says, 'Hey, we're over here getting our asses shot off, and all the Jews are back in the States making money.'"

Cohen slammed his carbine's bolt into place. He jammed the clip into the rifle and clicked a round into the chamber. He put the safety on. Then Cohen stood and approached the GI reading the newspaper. Several men were in the room, including Sergeant Tyrell.

Softly, Cohen said, "What did you say?"

"Then he repeated it," Cohen recalled many years later. "And I said, 'Well, I'm Jewish, and I'm not over there making money.' And he looked at me, and he said, 'You're not Jewish.' I said, 'What am I?' He said, 'You're Italian.' I said, 'I'm not Italian, and I don't give a damn what you are. We're all over here. If I ever hear you say anything about the Jews, I'll blow your head off.' And with that I lowered that muzzle right down to the center of his chest. Nobody ever said a word."

☆ ☆ ☆

When Sergeant Hubert J. Tyrell, the leader of Cohen's platoon, was awarded a battlefield commission, he was ordered to the rear. Tyrell's platoon remained in the field, living in the woods.

"We must have been up there about a week," Cohen recalled. "Oh, we were soaked and muddy and really filthy. Then this Jeep comes driving up. The lieutenant gets out in a brand new uniform and boots and shiny lieutenant's bars. We all jumped up and saluted him."

The erstwhile sergeant eyed his men. He was not a tall man, but the sharp new uniform with its lieutenant's bars looked impressive on him. Then he said, "The next guy who salutes me will be digging foxholes from here to Berlin. Don't anyone ever do that again."

"That's the kind of guy he was," Cohen said. "He would get a liquor ration and split it up. He would drink with us. When he was with you, nobody could get hurt."

☆ ☆ ☆

As the troops moved toward Berlin, town by town, their standing order was that if a building was taken the civilians had to be locked in the basement. German civilians were not thrilled with that procedure. Yes, their country was in the process of being conquered, but they resisted being herded underground.

"They gave us a bad time," Cohen said. "Then we found that the best way to do it was to tell them that the Russians were coming. You'd see the fear on their faces, and you had no problems with them."

☆ ☆ ☆

Cohen had grown up with his grandmother, Libby Strosberg, an immigrant from Russia. She'd spoken English, but she'd also spoken Yiddish, which is not radically different from German. His grandmother had used that language in conversations with Lillian Cohen whenever she'd wanted to say something that she didn't care to share with her grandson. As a child, Al Cohen had picked up enough Yiddish to understand bits and snatches of what German civilians were saying as the Allies moved through Germany. Other American soldiers of Polish ancestry spoke that language with some fluency. As the troops moved into German towns, they suddenly had people to talk to—Polish prisoners who'd been impressed as slave laborers in German war factories.

"We hit one town one night," Cohen recalled, "and the factory there must have been a clothing manufacturing plant, because we found a bunch of Hitler Youth uniforms. Some of the plants were small machine shops . . . the slave laborers were civilians. Some of them might have been, at one time, Polish soldiers. They wore civilian clothes. They were hardly fed. I would say that they weren't fed much better than the people in the concentration camps. . . . We were like gods to them. They'd been penned up in stockades, and—when freed—they'd go into town and help themselves. We wouldn't stop them. After a while, though, they came out with a directive that the slave laborers weren't to be let out until a military government unit moved in. So, we ended up having to guard those people, too."

☆ ☆ ☆

Cohen's group was a clean-up outfit. By the time they arrived in a town, the place had been suitably bombarded, and the tanks already had rolled through. The job of Cohen's outfit was to kill anybody left who still felt like fighting, as a good many Germans did.

"This one afternoon," he recalled, "they load up our platoon, put us in five Jeeps, and they wanted us to make contact with this other unit that was supposed to be in this fairly large town—more like a city, actually. So, we pile on the Jeeps, and we get to the town, and it's just about dusk, and we go up one of the main streets."

Along the route, German civilians were hanging white bedsheets from their windows as signs of surrender. Cohen's group happened on five SS troopers, who quickly surrendered. They were ordered to sit on the hoods of the Jeeps as the unit moved forward. At the intersection where they were to meet the other unit, Cohen's group found no one. Each Jeep then moved off in a different direction, searching for the unit with which they were to rendezvous.

In Cohen's Jeep were the driver, the radio operator, a medic, Lieutenant Tyrell and a Dutch soldier who'd been captured by the Germans and later freed by Allied forces as they moved through Germany. The Dutch soldier could have gone home, but he'd insisted on staying and fighting, so he and a few other Netherlanders ended up with Cohen's unit. They served mainly as interpreters.

The Jeep in which Cohen was riding pulled up in front of a church. The men realized that they could hear tanks nearby. They made the presumption, given the nature of their assignment, that the tanks were Shermans. Supposedly, this town had been cleared of Panzers and Tigers before their arrival. The church was a topic of special interest, however. Church steeples were sites favored by German snipers. The five SS troopers were hurriedly escorted at gunpoint to a nearby building and placed under guard.

"As we pull up," Cohen recalled, "we saw a couple of soldiers run into a building. It turned out to be the town hall. Everybody ran after them except our medic, Doc Jones, and I. I kept watching that church tower. The two of us are standing there by the Jeep, and we had the radio on the Jeep. We had the machine gun mounted on the dashboard of the Jeep. We had a bazooka in the trailer with all our ammunition, plus other stuff. And I see a man run out. I got him up against the wall, against one of the buildings, and he clicks his heels and goes, 'Heil Hitler.'"

The man was in civilian clothes, but Cohen found a pistol when he searched the prisoner, leading Cohen to believe that this man was not the civilian he was pretending to be. At that moment, a bazooka round thundered to the ground just past the Jeep. Cohen immediately ordered the medic into the town hall, where the rest of the Jeep's occupants had pursued the fleeing German soldiers.

"So," Cohen said years later, "I got rid of that Kraut that was there, and we ran into the building. We got in the front door, and there was a long hallway leading to the back door, and it was all doorways on the sides. We didn't even bother to look in the other rooms. Tyrell and the Dutchman take off down the street. They're going to look for this other outfit we're supposed to meet up with. So, they're gone about five minutes, and we hear a burst of machine gun fire. We thought that they'd bought it. About five minutes later, Tyrell comes back to the building. The Dutchman had been killed. He'd jumped in front of the lieutenant and saved his life."

After several minutes huddled in the town hall, trying to figure out what might be going on, the men made a run for the Jeep and got it rolling. They arrived back at the intersection to find that another Jeep had stopped there to set up a machine gun emplacement to fire on anything that might move along any of the roads that formed the intersection.

Convinced now that this town had not been properly cleared of opposition, the GI's began moving cautiously along the streets, eyes open for the enemy. Hearts pounding, they prowled with weapons ready, waiting to be attacked. Cohen hovered in a doorway near the intersection, looking for the unit he was to hook up with and looking, too, for more German soldiers. After 20 minutes, one of the other GI's came scurrying up the street. He'd happened upon a Tiger Royal, the largest and most ferocious German tank, prowling ominously along a nearby street.

"I guess they heard our tanks coming," Cohen recalled, "and we never did see it. They must have pulled it out of town. And then, little by little, our riflemen and the tanks and tank destroyers worked their way into town. But we lost that one man there."

☆ ☆ ☆

German civilians were hiding in basements—or in the woods outside town, or in caves in nearby forests. They'd fled to places they deemed less likely to be bombed or shelled than the towns in which they'd lived before the invasion. Moreover, once Americans moved into a town, German troops could be counted on to bombard the place at every opportunity.

Near Frankfurt, Cohen's unit had the machine guns set up near a set of railroad tracks, near an orchard. Cohen was manning the gun, keeping an eye on things, when another unit member appeared and told him that the lieutenant wanted him.

"So," Cohen said, "I got up, and he laid down behind

the machine gun. I got about 20 feet from him, and a mortar round came in. I hit the ground, and then I heard him hollering for the medic. Doc Jones comes running over to him, and the guy says, 'I'm hit.' And Doc Jones says, 'You're not hit. There's no blood.' The guy says, 'I tell you, goddammit, I'm hit.' Doc says, 'You're crazy. There's no blood.'"

The medic, known as Doc Jones, was Charles O. Jones of Sweatman, Ms. He cut away the man's fatigue pants. The GI had, indeed, been hit, superficially. The shrapnel had penetrated the skin but had severed no major blood vessels and broken no bones. Cohen got up and walked over to the scene.

"You son of a bitch," he told the wounded man. "You couldn't have shown up twenty seconds later, and I would have gotten hit, and I'd be back in the hospital and out of this."

All three men burst into uncontrollable laughter as they waited for the wounded man to be taken away by an ambulance. In that place at that time, humor was hard to come by, and the GI's took it where they could find it.

☆ ☆ ☆

Al Cohen had his own personal source of amusement. When guarding German soldiers, especially officers, he would move close to them and mutter, "Ich bin Juden." Translation: "I'm Jewish."

It was important to him that they know.

☆ ☆ ☆

At dusk one day, Cohen, his squad and another squad of machine gunners were climbing the side of a mountain. They presumed they were to find good ground for their guns, but the order to ascend the mountain had been issued without explanation, like so many other orders. Darkness fell so suddenly and sharply that each GI soon found himself holding on to the suspenders of the man ahead as the entire group struggled with machine guns, ammo crates and tripods, plus their regular assortment of personal combat weaponry, as they climbed.

"You're trying to be quiet," Cohen recalled. "We must have climbed for about four hours. You get up to the top, and there's a little level place. And we were all so tired and sweaty that we just set the gun up by laying it on the ground. So, I pulled the first watch, and everybody went to sleep."

Cohen was later relieved and drifted off to sleep on the ground. Just before dawn, a shroud of fog descended on the mountaintop. The GI manning the gun at that point found himself consumed by an urge to move his bowels. Proper procedure in such a circumstance called for the GI to awaken another soldier and then move off into the woods behind the machine gun. This man, however—perhaps lulled by the fog and the deceptive placidity of the scene—instead moved out from behind the machine gun and into the flat area in front of it.

"Not in back of the gun," Cohen recalled, "but in front of the gun. And he didn't know what was on the other side of the woods out there. He turns around with his back to the woods. He drops his pants, and he's relieving himself. And, as he's doing this, somebody comes up behind him, taps him on the shoulder and says, 'Du bist Deutch?' So, he jumps up, pulls up his pants and scrambles back to the gun, and he opens fire."

The sudden burst of machine gun fire awakened everybody—everybody, that is, except Al Cohen, who was deep in sleep. Even the explosion of gunfire all around failed to rouse him immediately from his slumber. Cohen later recalled, "I thought I was dreaming when I heard gunfire. So, I open my eyes as this is going on, and Doc Jones, our medic, is bending over me, and he's starting to write out a tag. He thought I got killed.

"When I sat up, it scared the hell out of him."

Rich Marowitz

RICHARD MAROWITZ

☆ ☆

Heavy vehicles roaring through and out of Marseilles' residential district carried Rich Marowitz and his comrades 20 miles to a barren, wind-swept hilltop known as Command Post 2.

"They packed us in two-and-a-half-ton trucks," Marowitz recalled decades later. "We had full packs and duffel bags. There were so many of us that you couldn't sit. We had to stand the whole time. We got there at night. It was a huge mountaintop—muddy, no trees, flat, nothing. We carried half a pup tent, so you always had to buddy up with somebody. We got up in the morning, and there were tents all over the place."

The sprawling tent city would be their home for the next 10 bitterly cold days and miserable, generally sleepless nights. For most of the green replacements, this was a rude awakening. Now, the war seemed unnervingly near. They were reminded constantly of its proximity by the nighttime blackouts and the boom of anti-aircraft guns firing from the port defenses at the occasional German interloper.

It was a busy time for the troops. Equipment was unpacked and cleaned. Weapons were made ready for war. Winter clothing was issued. These operations comprised the lion's share of their time. What spare time they had was spent trying to keep warm in the bitter winter weather. Hands were especially vulnerable in the freezing wind, especially after they had been scrubbed with gasoline. The routine was broken by the occasional 12-hour pass into town, where the Marseilles beggars struggled to separate young GI's from their cigarettes and money. To most GI's who got into town, the seaport bars constituted a welcome diversion from CP 2—although they quickly discovered that a sandwich purchased at the wrong place could cost a month's pay.

At CP 2, Captain McLaughlin approached Marowitz and asked him to take charge of the officer's mess. Marowitz wouldn't have to cook. His job would be to help serve the officers and ensure that everything ran properly.

"We had stew for a week straight," Marowitz recalled years later. "I asked the sergeant if we had anything else, and he told me peanut butter. I told him to put it in the stew. So, I bring it in and serve it to the officers. One of them says, 'Marowitz, what's in the stew?' And I say, 'Peanut butter.' They all look at me, and then the colonel says 'Well, I have to admit, it's a welcome change.' I just wiped my head and said, 'Whew!'"

A week after the Rainbow Division's infantry regiments arrived at CP 2, war news became a topic of intense interest as word of a German offensive began trickling in. The troops soon realized that they would not be engaged merely in an occupation mission. They also understood that Task Force Linden's original orders to serve as rear echelon support would now be modified to place them on the front lines. On December 19th, with the Battle of the Bulge in full swing, Marowitz and the rest of division's three infantry regiments were shipped north to engage the enemy. En route to the front, they were issued new orders to join the Seventh Army and relieve the 36th Infantry Division near the recently captured town of Strasbourg. No one knew at the time, but by New Year's Eve a new German offensive called Operation *Nordwind* would be launched in the south. Richard Marowitz with the 222nd—along with the 232nd and 242nd infantry regiments of Task Force Linden—would be thrust right into the midst of the battle.

By Christmas day, Marowitz and the 222nd Infantry had moved into position along the west bank of the Rhine near Strasbourg. For the next 10 days, they would be subject to a series of position shifts to cover for members of the Seventh Army who were being transferred to the beating, bleeding heart the Bulge. On January 4th, after more than a week of movement to plug holes all along the Rhine in the vicinity of Strasbourg, the 222nd Infantry was reassigned to the north-west—to an area near Soultz Sous Forets. Despite the region's designation as a quiet area, battles for possession of some small villages were still being waged.

On January 5th, after being relieved by the French First Army, the 232nd Infantry Regiment was beginning its reloca-tion from Strasbourg to Soultz when elements of the unit were caught in a German attack on the towns of Herrlishiem, Offendorf and Gambshien. This concentrated strike, carried out in pre-dawn darkness, caught the thinly spread green troops by surprise. Bolstered by tanks and artillery, the Germans initially overwhelmed the American defenders, cap turing and killing most of the soldiers defending the sur-rounded towns. Word of the German advance spread quickly, and portions of all three regiments of the Rainbow Division were divided into two task forces—Task Force A and Task Force B—to counterattack the enemy from Weyersheim to Gambshien. In two days of hard combat, the Rainbow Division stopped the enemy at the bridgehead. Less than a month after arriving on French soil, the GI's had succeeded in denying additional territory to an enemy who'd attacked in superior strength under ideal conditions.

To the north, the Germans would continue to probe at the first and third battalions of the 222nd Regiment only to be turned back at every attempt. For the next 15 days, the lines of defense would snake in a ballet of advance and retreat. A fierce, 52-hour battle at Hattan was a costly victory for the Rainbow. Two-thirds of the 33 officers and 748 men of the First Battalion were lost before being relieved by the Second Battalion. Nonetheless, after 18 days of engagement, the

Germans were stopped in their tracks by inexperienced Rainbow Division infantrymen. Months later, a captured Nazi intelligence officer who'd fought at Hatten lauded the division's fighting capabilities. A German tank officer, who said that combat at Hattan was more ferocious than anything he'd experienced—including during his three years on the Eastern front—echoed that sentiment. The new Rainbow Division acquitted itself as admirably in battle as its famous predecessor had during the First World War, and on ground eerily similar to that soaked with the blood of their namesake decades before.

Rich Marowitz was attached to 222nd Infantry Headquarters Company. He was never far from the front, but he'd spent his time working the officer's mess and doing odd jobs that centered mostly on packing and moving the unit command post as the front line contracted and expanded with enemy attempts at penetration. Command was usually stationed about 250 yards behind the line—far enough to be out of the direct line of fire but close enough to be easily overrun by a rapidly advancing force. The command post's vulnerability would be vividly illustrated on the night of January 20th.

With the Battle of the Bulge having turned in favor of the Americans to the north and the Germans now retreating back behind the Sigfried Line, Hitler was more determined than ever to mount a successful attack in the southern sector. The German goal was now to capture Haguenau and the adjacent road network to permit their armor easy access to tank country to the south. The idea was to enable the Panzers to drive the Allied forces back to the Vosges Mountains.

On January 20th, in the midst of a fierce blizzard, Marowitz was again packing up Headquarters Company for relocation along the Moder River, northwest of Haguenau. To most, the new order to withdraw back to the river had the feel of retreat. The American troops were sharing the ice-encrusted roads with newly liberated French, now carrying their possessions on their backs in an effort to escape the German advance. As a one-star general said to the newly blooded members of the Rainbow, "You guys are so green you don't know when to back up."

Having fought so hard to stop the enemy, the Rainbow soldiers were pained to give up ground that had cost so much. With snow falling and the troops moving slowly in sub-freezing temperatures, a few squads were left behind to cover the retreat and convince the Germans that the area was still being defended.

"We just got out of there barely ahead of the Krauts," Marowitz said decades later. "The roads were so bad you could barely walk two feet without falling down. That was a close one."

The 222nd Infantry, Marowitz's outfit, settled into the Ohlungen Forest between Schweighausen and Neubourg on the other side of the Moder River. With one battalion held in reserve, two battalions of the 222nd covered a front of 7,500 yards—an area large enough, under normal circumstances, to require a full division. The Moder River, 20 feet across at its widest and only five feet deep, posed only a modest obstacle to attackers. The sparse forest offered limited cover. The snow was waist deep and the temperature below freezing as the men of the 222nd waited motionless in their soaked foxholes. Their fellow Rainbow Division regiment, the 232nd, flanked them on the left, and the 314th Infantry covered their right.

The GI's knew that the Germans were coming. They had no way of knowing that the brunt of the attack would be directed at the heart of the 222nd. The American infantrymen would be outnumbered over 5-1 at the point of attack as five regiments—including elements of the German Seventh Parachute Division, 25th Panzer Division and the 47th Volksgrenadier Division—would lead the charge. At 1800 hours on January 24th, enemy artillery began sailing in. For the next two hours the ground shook as the GI's gamely held their positions. The German artillery quickly knocked out Rainbow communications. In that rugged, wooded terrain the only consistent—albeit, fragmented—reports were coming in by foot messenger. Shortly after the barrage, the shrouded silhouettes of German infantry appeared through the forest as the first wave of attackers forded the Moder and launched the assault. The Americans responded with a field of devastating fire from their water-soaked foxholes, and the first wave was repulsed.

Marowitz, just behind the front with the 222nd Headquarters Company, was manning his weapon as isolated reports arrived of Germans penetrating the line. Close-range fighting made artillery useless. Men of the thinly spread 222nd were cut off in places, but they continued to fight as the Germans forced a gap between companies and poured troops through it. The resistance confounded the Germans. They realized that the men of the 222nd were isolated, and they wondered why the GI's refused to surrender. For the next night and a day the fighting raged as the Germans would thrust and retreat, gaining ground in the forest, but never able to break out of it. By the evening of the 25th, it was determined that the German advance had been completely repulsed by the 222nd. German losses were estimated at 800 dead, an undetermined number of wounded and 112 captured. The 222nd had suffered 18 dead, 146 wounded and 74 reported missing in action. A planned attack by the Allies on the morning of the 26th did nothing more than reestablish the original front, as the Germans had retreated during the night back across the Moder River. Their gallantry in battle would earn the men of the 222nd a Presidential Unit Citation, the U.S. Army's second highest wartime honor.

On January 27th, the 222nd was relieved by elements of the 101st Airborne Division. The exhausted warriors of the 222nd were trucked back some 60 miles into the Loraine area of France for some R&R. The towns had been devastated, but the bombed-out buildings were still better than foxholes. For the first time in a month, the men of the 222nd were warm, dry and able to consume hot meals.

Marowitz easily communicated with people in the Loraine area because they spoke a mixed dialect of German and French, which Marowitz could emulate through a combination of high school French and Yiddish. He ran into Captain

McLaughlin, who noted that Marowitz was wearing a uniform that looked like it just came out of a magazine. The uniform was perfectly pressed with creases that Marowitz later described as "so sharp you could cut your finger on." The captain asked how Marowitz managed to look so sharp under such horrific conditions. Bribery, Marowitz explained.

"Tell me about it," the captain said.

Years later, Marowitz recalled, "I told him I have women lined up to do my laundry, and the bribery consists of soap. The captain asked if he could get in on this, and I said sure. So he scribbles something on a piece of paper and tells me to go to the supply hut and see the sergeant. The sergeant reads the paper and asks me what I was up to. I had this reputation as a wheeler-dealer. He asked who it was signed by, and I told him the captain and he could call him if he wanted. Finally, he handed me a whole case of soap. . . . I took it back to the captain, and he told me, 'Anytime you need soap, just come and get it.' It didn't help my reputation, but the officers went along with it. The guys got a kick out of it. They used to say that I got away with things most guys would get thrown in jail for."

Two weeks later, the Rainbow was ordered back to the front to replace the 45th Infantry Division in the Hardt Mountains northwest of Haguenau. This was to be a defensive mission, but it included a vigorous schedule of patrols and raids to determine enemy strength. The 222nd was responsible for four miles of an eight-mile front near the town of Wingen sur Moder. It was heavily wooded country. The infantrymen set up housekeeping in their foxholes, which included mining the area in front and setting up trip wires to ensnare enemy invaders. Most of the men not on the front, including Marowitz, were billeted in French homes or found shelter in abandoned buildings.

The Germans had laid thousands of mines in the area, mostly small explosives called "Shu" mines designed to blow off legs or shatter feet. The 139 reconnaissance patrols that were run during the last two weeks of February were concerned more with the those mines than with enemy fire. In the first few days, the area was also the target of German artillery. Shells would explode in the treetops—"tree bursts," they were called—and send fiery splinters raining down.

The U.S. patrols enjoyed heavy artillery support. If a German opened fire, he would soon find himself under a rain of death. The patrols and constant shelling were taking their toll on the Germans. Many deserted their units and surrendered. One prisoner remarked, "It got so bad that we'd rather retreat than open fire on patrols." During this period, U.S. artillery began using "secret shells." These were shells with radar devices in the nose that could be set off a pre-determined distance above the ground, increasing the field of destruction. Moreover, a campaign to encourage German surrenders was introduced. Artillery and mortar attacks often were followed by leaflet drops and radio broadcasts urging the enemy to give up.

Marowitz had helped set up the command headquarters in Wingen, but he was wearying of his menial tasks, errands and occasional turns with the bugle. He asked Captain McLaughlin for a change of assignment. Life behind the line had gotten almost cushy, featuring showers, movies and clean clothing. Even the men on the front line were enjoying two hot meals a day. On a few occasions, cans of beer were delivered to their foxholes. The weather had been horrendous during December and January, but it was improving. Although there was no shortage of rain and mud, temperatures were rising. The captain asked Marowitz if he could handle a .50-cal. machine gun. I can take one apart and put it together again, Marowitz lied.

"Okay," Captain McLauglin said, "you're the new machine gunner on my Jeep."

What Marowitz didn't realize was that Captain McLaughlin was an action junkie, and the officer was now in a position to feed his addiction. While stationed in Wingen, the captain would order his driver, Private Flatt, to take routes dangerously close to enemy lines—or even to cross them. On a few occasions, with Marowitz manning the Jeep's machine gun, they would run into the intelligence and reconnaissance patrols that were probing up to 2,000 yards inside the German front.

"I remember one time in Wurzburg," Marowitz recalled decades later, "I was out with the captain. We were supposedly looking for a new command post, as we were on the more forward at that time, and there was lots of street-to-street fighting in the area. So, we turn the corner at this one street, and this sergeant stops the Jeep and says we can't go down there 'cause there's fighting in this block. So, the captain points to the bars on his collar, and the sergeant steps out of the way and off we go. Well, we don't go half a block and there's a sniper firing at us. So, the three of us go piling out of the Jeep and behind this little two-foot brick wall. The captain asks if we knew where the sniper was. Flatt, the driver, says, 'Across the street.' And the captain says, 'Where across the street?' I tell him it sounded high, and I think the guy's behind the chimney on that building. He asks if I can get to the .50-cal., and I told him, 'If you give me some cover.' So, he and Flatt crawl to the end of the wall and start laying down cover fire. I run to the Jeep and take aim at the chimney. I always kept the gun loaded with armor-piercing ammunition, so it cut right through the brick and took care of the sniper. I said to the captain, 'Did you have your fun today?' He said, 'Get in the Jeep. Flatt, take us home.' He was satisfied."

On March 13th, word came down that the Seventh Army was to attack into Germany in two days. The Rainbow Division was again at full strength, having been joined by the rest of the units that had arrived in February from Camp Gruber. The Rainbow finally was going on its first offensive of the war. The mission was to attack through the Hardt Mountains, take the higher ground and then break through the Sigfried Line and continue until the division had reached Austria. The advance made significant progress the first two days, with only light casualties for the 222nd. Getting bogged down in the mountains the third day generated some angst.

There was no clear supply line and little water, but the speed of the operation had given the retreating Germans little time to stop and mount a defense.

By March 19th, the Rainbow Division had reached the Dragon's Teeth and the west wall pillboxes of the Sigfried Line. Patton's Third Army had already smashed through to the north and was racing to the Rhine. The next day, an attack was ordered. On March 21st, a major artillery and close support aircraft bombardment began battering the line. Shellfire poured down on the fortifications. While the shelling didn't destroy the forts, it did destroy German morale. Once the bombing stopped, the 222nd Infantry began its assault. Some Germans ran; others surrendered. Only token resistance at the Sigfried Line gave the GI's an opportunity to catch the enemy in the roads and on the mountains before they could make their escape. Planes were called in to bomb fleeing forces in concert with a day and night artillery barrage. Entire columns were slaughtered. Roads were strewn with dead men and horses along with the wreckage of vehicles, wagons and other equipment. In a war in which most gains had been measured in yards, the Rainbow Division had advanced 15 miles and taken 2,000 prisoners in only 24 hours.

As March ended, the Rainbow was on the move over the Rhine and, to their surprise, meeting very little enemy resistance. The GI's had been warned against fraternization, since they were now in the home territory of a dangerous enemy. What was amazing to most of the Americans was how much Hitler had accomplished all by himself. It seemed he had conquered most of Europe single-handedly, since all the Germans interviewed told the soldiers how much they hated the Furher and had never supported the Nazi Party. German civilians in small villages were very supportive of the American GI's. Citizens of cities that had incurred heavy damage were different. They tended to blame the Allies for the devastation, although none admitted to being a Nazi.

Once inside the Fatherland, American soldiers were no longer required to live in bombed-out houses or abandoned public buildings. Civilian homes were requisitioned as the owners were rousted and told to go live with relatives. GI's who'd lived in frozen foxholes now slept in German feather beds.

The Rainbow Division's next big obstacle was the city of Wurzburg. The city could not be taken without days of bitter street-to-street fighting. Citizens took up arms against the invaders, whom Nazi propaganda had portrayed as gangsters and hoodlums. Nearly every building contained a sniper. Police officers and fire-fighter joined the Wehrmacht in defense of the city. The assault was made more difficult by a network of underground tunnels that permitted the defenders to retreat and reappear behind the Americans.

During the Wurzburg siege, Captain McLaughlin, with Flatt at the wheel and Marowitz behind the .50-cal. machine gun, would continue his unauthorized forays into dangerous areas. As houses, commercial buildings and tunnels were cleared of resistance, one by one, and the city taken, Marowitz would opt to move on from his machine gun duties with the captain and volunteer for a far more perilous assignment. It was a decision Marowitz made as the Rainbow closed in on Munich, Hitler's home for so many years.

And the cradle of the Nazi Party.

German Panzer tanks
(*Associated Press Photo*)

RICHARD MAROWITZ

☆ ☆

Rich Marowitz—bugler, officers' mess boss and machine gunner on the Jeep of a officer with a thirst for action—had his eye on new duty in the U.S. Army.

He was pondering membership in an I and R unit. I and R is military code for Intelligence and Reconnaissance. GI's in I and R units acted as point scouts for their divisions or regiments. They would report in the early morning to the Command Post, pick up maps and get briefed on the day's mission. That usually would mean slipping into hostile territory and gathering information on enemy size, strength and location.

"The I and R's job was to find the enemy and report back," Marowitz explained years later. "How is it that the enemy always found them first? When your job is to drive a Jeep down the middle of the road, you are going to be seen first. They were living targets. It's no wonder the turnover rate was so high."

At full strength the I and R platoon attached to Headquarters Company of the 222nd Regiment consisted of two squads—12 men to a squad, traveling in six Jeeps, four men to a Jeep. In addition, the platoon had a command Jeep carrying a lieutenant, a sergeant, a driver and a machine gunner. When traveling in formation, the last Jeep was called the "getaway" Jeep. In the event of an enemy attack, the job of the getaway Jeep was to escape and bring back help.

I and R's procedure was to move ahead of the main force, slip into a town or city, get out of the Jeeps and move on foot to assess the resistance. The I and R platoon would then clear the area house-by-house and building-by-building. Once an area was clear, they would climb back into their Jeeps, head on to the next potential enemy sanctuary and repeat the routine. Most of the time, I and R was the first unit to enter small villages or wooded areas—to probe for enemy snipers or panzerfaust (bazookas). It was anxious and dangerous work.

The I and R platoon's turnover rate was around 75 per cent. They often were referred to by other GI's as "suicide squads." After the war, an I and R unit member asked another GI in communications why he'd refused to speak to any members of the scouting platoon. The communications GI said, "I didn't want to get to know any of you guys because I didn't want to get to like you. I knew every time you went out the chances were good you weren't coming back."

The loss of I and R men was heavy during April 1945. The 222nd Regiment I and R platoon, on patrol near the city of Wertheim, got into a heavy skirmish on the first of the month. Four GI's were killed, five wounded and five captured. What was left of the unit reported that they'd sighted the enemy. The rest of the regiment gathered up their guns and lit out in hot pursuit.

Commanders were looking for volunteers to fill the vacant slots. Marowitz decided that if he was going into enemy territory anyway, he might as well be with a group of people who knew what they were doing. When Captain McLaughlin got word of his decision, he asked Marowitz why he wanted that job, since he probably would get killed doing it. In his mind, Marowitz acknowledged that reality. Still, he'd concluded that joining a unit with a 75 per cent casualty rate was far safer than continuing to accompany McLaughlin on the captain's unsanctioned action safaris.

"We were always getting shot at when we were out with the captain," Marowitz recalled in later years. "I just felt that being a target of one in 28 was better odds than one in three."

In early April, as the Allies closed in on Berlin, everything was moving quickly. The Rainbow had cleared Wurzburg after three days of intense street-to-street fighting. The next major target was the city of Schweinfurt. Along the way, small towns like Dettlebach, Bibergau and Effeldorf were taken after brief but intense bouts of combat. The German plan was clear—leave behind token resistance along the way to the major cities and then hunker down and offer stiff opposition on the outskirts and in the hearts of major urban centers.

The I and R platoon was always at the tip of the action, although it was not always only the enemy they had to be concerned with. Sometimes they would find themselves so far out in front of the regiment that air reconnaissance would mistake them for Germans and call in artillery strikes on them. On one occasion when I and R was already dodging friendly fire, German Tiger tanks also spotted them. Marowitz and his comrades immediately came under fire from both sides. The platoon rolled out of their Jeeps and tried to burrow into any ground depression they could find, making themselves as flat as possible and then hanging on as they bounced in the dirt with each falling shell. The unit commander that day was a Lieutenant Short. Using a 694 radio, he identified the platoon and redirected the U.S. artillery strike at the German tanks.

"It was something to watch as the tanks played it perfectly," Marowitz said years later. "First the artillery would drop in front of the tanks, and the spotter—Lieutenant Short, in this case—would tell them to fire further back. And the tanks would move forward into the spot where the shells just hit. They would just keep moving back and forth, but some of the artillery guys knew this maneuver and would leave some guns aimed in the same spot, and eventually they got them."

Standard equipment for each I and R Jeep was one

.30-cal. machine gun and an M-1 rifle for each of the four riders. Only the command Jeep carried a 694 radio, one powerful enough to contact headquarters or call in artillery strikes. That's the equipment the book called for, at any rate. In actual practice, though, I and R units scavenged as much firepower and communications equipment as they could carry—including 300 radios for all Jeeps as well as bazookas, 60 MM mortars and other non-issue weapons. The GI's understood that being able to stay in contact and make huge noise, if necessary, was vital to their survival.

So was speed of action. Of the four men who rode in each Jeep, only the driver kept his legs inside the vehicle. All the passengers rode with legs hung over the side. In case of attack, they would pour out of the Jeep like a fountain and roll into any nearby ditch. The driver drove with the choke and his foot near the brake. At the point of engagement, he would hit the choke, stalling the Jeep, and jam a foot on the brake as he grabbed his rifle and rolled out for cover.

"Nobody ever got hurt," Marowitz remembered. "We were the fastest getter-outers of Jeeps in the war."

Sometimes, however, rolling out of the Jeep and ducking wasn't an option. During one mission, Marowitz's I and R platoon rounded a bend and came face-to-face with 50 German soldiers with horse-drawn carts.

"Now who do you think was more surprised?" Marowitz recalled many decades later. "Both! The fighting breaks out, and on this particular day I had an M-1 carbine that I had taken off a guy who didn't need it any more. The carbine is shorter and lighter than the M-1 rifle. There was a German in the ditch, and I came down with my gun as he went up with his and—click!—it misfires. I thought I was dead, but one of guys behind me took care of business. When it was over, I took that carbine and threw it as far as I could."

The attack on Schweinfurt began on April 10th, preceded by a massive artillery and bombing barrage aimed at destroying enemy armor installations and escape routes out of the city. When the Rainbow entered, many buildings had been leveled, but the famed ball bearing plants of Schweinfurt were still operating—albeit at only 30 per cent capacity and manned by slave labor. Husky Polish and Russian women, freed of their slavery, emerged from bomb shelters and hugged American soldiers in the streets. During the mop-up stages of the siege on April 13th, word arrived that President Franklin D. Roosevelt had died of a stroke in Georgia. Throughout the division, spontaneous memorial services were held to honor the fallen leader. Despite Roosevelt's loss, however, there remained a war to fight, and the Rainbow was moving on to the adjoining cities of Furth and Nurnberg.

Since Wurzburg, the Rainbow had cleared 100 square miles of Nazi territory and captured more than 50 towns and villages, taking over 6,600 prisoners in the process. In Furth, a population center of about 100,000, fierce fighting raged for hours. Four other outfits joined the Rainbow in the operation—including the 45th Infantry, Third Infantry, Fourth Infantry and the 12th Armored Division. Again, as in Schweinfurt, massive bombings and shelling jarred the city, followed by the infantry moving in to root the enemy out of every gutted dwelling and cellar. As the defense was pushed from Furth east into the still larger city of Nurnberg, the process was repeated. In one day, the Rainbow captured 1,907 prisoners, the largest one-day total of the war.

For the next few days, the regiment continued to push south. On April 21st, the Rainbow went into reserve to catch up on sleep and take care of general housekeeping until April 25th. The next day the division fought its way over the Danube, meeting heavy SS resistance at the town of Donauworth. The Rainbow was now sweeping toward the last major obstacle of the campaign, Munich. In the path lay several villages, including one that lodged forever in the mind of every soldier who saw it—a place called Dachau.

On the morning of April 29th, Marowitz and the full I and R platoon received their orders and were sent out to Dachau post haste. All contact would be by radio. I and R would not be reporting back because the entire division would be following. Accompanying the unit were two prisoners of war who'd agreed to point out mines along the way. As the mission continued, Marowitz remembered, the radio kept going off, asking for coordinates and admonishing the I and R men for moving too slowly. Unbeknownst to the I and R platoon, they were in a race, and the prize was Dachau. The Rainbow was in competition with the Third and 45th Divisions to reach the town first. Had anyone known what would be waiting there, reaching Dachau first would not have been considered a victory.

The soldiers in the front of the patrol would stop if they saw heavy cover or woods and investigate before continuing. This was procedure, but there would be no race won this day following procedure. Finally, Lt. Short, the platoon commander, stopped the Jeep and told the men that, based on transmissions he was receiving, they had two choices. They could continue by the book and lose the race or step on the gas and go like hell.

"We all decided we would step on the gas," Marowitz recalled. "We tossed the German prisoners off the Jeeps and took off. We didn't need them anyway. Nobody puts mines in the middle of a paved road, where we traveled. They usually put them on the shoulder. If they did plant one in the road, you could see where the pavement had been disturbed."

Marowitz's unit was flying at top speed toward Dachau. At one point, they went right through a German column at a crossroads. Jumping on their .30-cal. machine guns, the I and R men loosed bursts of automatic fire as they roared right past the surprised German soldiers, who went diving off the road. The same situation arose with other Germans on a parallel road—with similar results. The lieutenant contacted the division trailing behind to inform them of the enemy strength and location, so they could mop them up on the way.

The I and R platoon was fired on as it approached a small village. The GI's rolled out of their Jeeps. Carrying as much firepower as they could manage, they set up a position on a small knoll and let loose on the town with everything they had. The lieutenant then shouted, "Three men assault the town."

"I thought that was the most comical order I had ever heard," Marowitz recalled. "Anyway, it was Larry Hancock and Herb Herman and me, and we went down and cleared the first few houses and waved the rest of the guys in."

The clearing of houses or buildings usually consisted of banging on the door. If the knock elicited no response, the GI's would toss a grenade inside, then investigate to see if anybody was left alive. Later, in a building on the way to Dachau, the men noticed a trap door on the floor move slightly as they entered. Raising the door, they found a full cellar of German soldiers, who were only too happy to surrender.

"As we started to clear the town and pick up prisoners they were coming out of the woodwork," Marowitz recalled. "We were breaking up weapons and telling them to put their hands on their head and start walking back up the road. They looked at us like we were crazy, but there were over a 150 of them and we didn't have time to fool with them. We had to get going."

As they barreled through another village, the GI's were attacked by a German with a bazooka hiding behind a bush. The missile sailed over Marowitz's head, and the concussion blew him and his comrades out of the Jeep. Soldiers in the trailing Jeep used their .30-cal. machine gun to dispatch the sniper.

"So we got up to get back in the Jeep," Marowitz said, "and I felt something sticking out of my leg. It was a little piece of shrapnel, a little thing. Herb was yelling to get Pete [the platoon medic]. I said, 'For what?' And he said to report it. I said, 'Get back in the Jeep.' That was stupid because I would have got a Purple Heart, and that was worth five points. We went home based on a point system, and I could have gone home sooner."

As the I and R platoon approached Dachau, they were assailed by the rancid stench of rotting flesh. They presumed that the odor arose from decaying carcasses of farm animals or horses who'd fallen victim to bombs or artillery fire. Such corpses littered the countryside. As they approached the town, which also housed an SS training facility and a camp for prisoners, they were bombarded by heavy artillery, including German 88's. Marowitz and the rest of the I and R unit abandoned their Jeeps for the relative safety of a nearby ditch and waited for the rest of the division to show up. Finally, as the regiment approached from the rear, an American M-4 Sherman tank came rolling out of the town. As Marowitz and his companions rose from their cover, the tank turned and aimed its cannon at them.

"We thought it was one of ours that had come into town from another direction," Marowitz recalled. "It was really a captured Sherman. It was the second time that I really thought I was dead, but before he could fire, one of our tank destroyers took it out. They knew that there were no American tanks in Dachau. I went over and kissed that tank destroyer."

For the next several hours, the SS troops who hadn't fled the night before put up a brave battle, but the Rainbow finally overwhelmed them with the help of the 33,000 prisoners incarcerated at Dachau. As American troops entered the concentration camp, the inmates went wild with joy, hugging GI's and trying to get soldiers to sign autographs. The inmates also attacked the remaining SS troops, some of whom had exchanged their black uniforms for prison garb in hopes of avoiding capture.

The camp inmates were living skeletons—starved and hollow-eyed. The camp's stench was overpowering. The GI's quickly realized that what they had thought from a distance had been dead animals turned out to be thousands of human corpses. Some of the victims had been shot. Some had been gassed. Others had simply starved to death. The Germans had run out of coal to cremate the bodies, so they'd simply just stacked the dead in buildings. Until just a few days before the camp's capture, the Nazis had been busy executing up to 200 prisoners a day.

The horror of the scene was gut-wrenching. On railroad tracks at the camp, the Rainbow men found 40 boxcars, each containing about 30 bodies of prisoners who'd been starved or shot. The "Death Train" had arrived from another concentration camp in Buchenwald, and the camp at Dachau had been unable to accommodate the new inmates. So, with the Americans approaching, the SS guards had left the inmates in the cars until they'd died. Inmates who'd managed to open the boxcar doors had been machine-gunned.

By the time the camp was liberated, only one man in 1,500 was found alive in the boxcars. Many of the prisoners freed that day were in such bad shape that they lasted only a few more hours. What they saw at Dachau shocked and stunned the Rainbow men. It was confirmation that they were fighting against a unique and profoundly unprincipled tyranny that desperately needed to be destroyed.

The Rainbow spent little time amid the horrors of Dachau. Spurred by a renewed hatred of Nazism, they charged toward Bavaria. As they closed in on Munich, the Bavarian capital, I and R got a special assignment. Two German civilians had been supplying information to the Allies and had revealed the location of Hitler's Munich apartment. Marowitz and one I and R squad—three Jeeps and 12 men— were dispatched with the Germans to locate and search the premises.

Arriving at Munich, the only passage the GI's could find intact over the Isar River was a foot bridge at the top of a long, wide concrete stairway. The Jeeps were put in four-low gear and climbed the bumpy stairway. With only a few inches of tire clearance on each side, they traversed the narrow bridge. After descending an identical stairway on the other side, the Jeeps crawled through the quiet, seemingly deserted streets of Munich to Adolf Hitler's personal residence. Answering the banging on the door was a tall, matronly, English housekeeper, who demanded to know why everyone was so angry at poor Mr. Hitler, who was such a fine man.

As Marowitz recalled the incident, "Herb Herman, who was with me, said, 'Rich, I'm gonna throw her down the stairs.'

I said, 'Forget it. Let's do what we have to do and get out of here.' It felt really weird there. It was late morning or early afternoon, just before our troops arrived. We started to search the house. Everyone split up and went into different rooms. I went into Hitler's bedroom—of course, I didn't know it at the time. His personal stuff had been removed. I opened the closet, and I saw something dark up on the shelf. So, I dragged a chair over and climbed up. Reaching in, I pulled out this gorgeous top hat. Inside the hat, in big gold letters, were the initials 'A. H.' I swear to this day that I could still see his head in that hat. I was still so pissed off at what I saw in Dachau that I threw the hat on the floor and stomped the hell out of it. Now, I don't remember this, but Herb Herman said I came out of the bedroom with this hat on my head strutting like Charlie Chaplin. It ended up in the bottom of my duffel bag."

A few hours later, the Rainbow captured Munich without resistance. It was a wild scene. Fully a quarter of Munich's population was made up of slave laborers, including hundreds of British and American prisoners of war eager for revenge on those who'd profited from their toil. Many Munich citizens, smarting from bullying and beatings by the SS troops who'd garrisoned the city, also welcomed the American liberators. For them, Munich's capture marked an end to life below ground, huddling in terror in the face of the countless Allied bombings that had reduced much of the city to rubble.

After restoring some semblance of order by driving looters away from warehouses, posting guards and rounding up prisoners, the Rainbow was freed to continue its advance south to Austria. After Munich, however, the war seemed unofficially over. Droves of German soldiers continued to turn themselves into the Americans. Word of the German government's surrender came as no surprise to the Rainbow men.

A week before the surrender, on the same day the I and R squad was poking around Hitler's Munich residence, the Fuhrer committed suicide in his bunker. Nearly 60 years later, when asked if he realized that the Fuhrer's suicide had occurred on that day, Marowitz replied, "Absolutely. When Hitler found out that a skinny Jewish kid from Brooklyn had stomped all over his top hat, he killed himself."

Rich Marowitz and Hitler's hat

DOUG VINK

☆ ☆

As the Fighting Turtles rolled northward, edging ever nearer to the Dragon's Teeth at the German border, resistance stiffened. The breakout from Bastogne had been relatively uneventful for most of the Sixth Armored Division—the Sad Sack being a conspicuous exception. Now, however, artillery shells began falling on the advancing Shermans. German infantry appeared in force, attacking with mortars and bazookas. Panzers were everywhere, with their thick armor and big guns.

"They weren't beaten," Doug Vink recalled years later. "They still had plenty of fight left in them."

The Shermans engaged the Panzers in cavalry tactics perfected by the Plains Indians against the U.S. Army nearly a century earlier. A Sherman would serve as a decoy—showing itself to the enemy, running off immediately and luring the Panzer into pursuit. The idea was to lead the bigger, meaner fighting machine past a hill or building or a stand of trees where other Shermans were lurking, waiting to take out the Panzer with cannon fire from the side or rear. Machine for machine, the Panzers were vastly deadlier than the Shermans, but now there were many Shermans moving toward the Dragon's Teeth and an increasingly smaller number of Panzers to stop them. Slowly but surely, what the Germans referred to as "panther tanks" were being overrun by a relentless herd of fighting turtles.

Even at close range, the best a Sherman could hope for was a shot from the 75 MM cannon that would disable the Panzer. Then, as the German crew poured from the tank clutching small arms, they would be mowed down by .50-cal. and .30-cal. machine gun fire. Or, if the German crew stayed with the Panzer to return fire with its 88 MM cannon, the Shermans would close in for the kill, firing their 75s in hope of igniting the Panzer's gas tank.

"Most of the time," Doug Vink recalled decades later, "they burned just like we did when they hit us."

Occasionally, in an area thick with Panzers, the Shermans would simply leave the wounded, immobile German tank and move on to engage the next enemy. Soon the Allied infantry would be coming up behind, armed with bazookas and mortars, to finish off the German crew members. Because German tanks generally fell to the efforts of not just one Sherman crew but of several, and because the infantry was on hand so often to finish the job, tank crews tended not to keep tallies of their kills. Fighter pilots might display their victories on the sides of their planes, but tankers had little down time for decorating their fighting machines. Moreover, they were discouraged by their commanders from keeping records. A tank crew that advertised its skill at killing enemy tanks was not a tank crew that could expect gentle treatment if captured on the battlefield.

The Sixth Armored Division crossed rivers on pontoon bridges. The 25th Engineers followed the Fighting Turtles. When water was to be crossed, the engineers would move forward and erect a bridge with great dispatch. Then the tanks would roll.

"If you want a special sensation," Vink said, "you want to cross a pontoon bridge in a medium tank. You went up and down and up and down, and back and forth, and you were worried every second that the thing was going to snap. You would go across one tank at a time, and when one got three-quarters of the way across another tank would start behind you. . . . No closed hatches on those trips. You were ready to jump out any second."

The engineers went into action again as the Fighting Turtles finally arrived at the Dragon's Teeth. The obstacles protruded from the Earth, sharp concrete points aimed at the gray winter sky. The tankers studied the Dragon's Teeth as the engineers moved forward with explosives.

"You look at those things," Vink recalled, "and you wondered, 'How the hell are we going to get a tank through them?' Tanks can climb, but the way these things were situated, you would get up in the air, and the next tooth would be in a slightly different position, and it would drop you to one side, and you would get hung up. Once you got off the track, you were done. Then the engineers came up and blew out a section of them, and we got through."

Once through the Dragon's Teeth, the Sad Sack's steel tracks finally dug into German soil, rolling toward Berlin and the leadership of the Nazi party. On Good Friday 1945, they approached a German town and pulled off the road, taking a breather.

"On Sunday," Vink recalled, "The civilians in the town came out with hard-boiled eggs, colored, and different food for us. This was the Germans. And that's where I lost my reputation of being a good machine gunner. I fired at three German soldiers running across a field and didn't touch any one of them. That also was where we picked up three German prisoners."

One of the German women who'd come out of town confided to the tankers that three German soldiers were hiding in her cellar. Vink and another tanker promptly grabbed their weaponry, Vink latching onto his sawed-off Thompson submachine gun. They then walked into town, found the woman's house and called down into the basement for the three to surrender. Knowing that resistance was likely to result in a hand grenade rolling down into the enclosed area, two uniformed men emerged from the basement—or, more accurately, one man and a boy of about 16. The man was about 65, part of the German home guard. As they came out into the open, hands held high, Vink could hear their sergeant still in the basement shouting angry orders at the two prisoners. Ultimately, however, the sergeant also emerged from the cellar. Vink studied him carefully. The sergeant in command, Vink estimated, was about 15 years old, a Hitler Youth member left to die in combat for the Third Reich.

These were members of the *Volksturm*, a last-ditch defense force put together by the Nazis to defend the Fatherland as the Allies closed in and the regular German army collapsed. The *Volksturm* was composed of older men and boys deemed unfit for regular service but, for the most part, fully prepared to kill and be killed as their country was overrun.

"We took them back to where the tank was," Vink recalled, "and tied them to trees. There was only four of us in the tank that day. We didn't have a tank commander with us. . . . That put me in command of the tank."

His first responsibility now, Vink realized, was getting rid of these prisoners. As various Allied vehicles rolled by, he pleaded with the drivers to take the three prisoners off his hands. No one would comply. These guys are your problem, Vink was told. Meanwhile, the 15-year-old sergeant, tied to his tree, raged incessantly in German at the American tankers. The elderly home guard soldier could speak some English, but every time he tried to speak to his captors the youthful sergeant would roar at him, and he would immediately shut up. After a few days of this, and eager to get his tank rolling again, Vink found that the boy sergeant was getting on his nerves in a serious way. Finally an Allied ambulance came by. Take these guys off our hands, Vink pleaded.

"Are they wounded?" the ambulance driver demanded.

Vink said, "Oh, do they have to be—real bad?"

"No," the ambulance driver said. "If they're bleeding, I'll take them."

Vink approached the mouthy teenage sergeant and smacked him in the head with the sawed-off butt of the Thompson. Blood gushed. Then Vink turned to the ambulance driver.

"Is he bleeding enough?" Vink asked.

"Looks like it to me," the driver said. "Put 'em in the back."

Further down the road toward Berlin, Vink's tank caught up with the rest of his outfit. The Fighting Turtles had moved into Germany with great speed. Finally, they'd outrun their orders. Now, the tanks were sitting in trees by the side of the road awaiting instructions on where to go next. Vink pulled the Sad Sack off to the shoulder.

"They were going to send us in another direction," Vink recalled, "and all of a sudden we were being strafed by a fighter plane. It turned out to be one of our own. We all jumped on our 50 calibers and fired back at him."

The Sixth Armored had moved into the Fatherland with such speed that they'd received no orders on which color panel to affix to their Shermans to identify them as Allied tanks. The American P-51 pilot, moving in from an air base at the rear, had mistakenly identified them as German fighting machines. Caught up in the fog of war, the tankers of the Sixth Armored instantly realized that the only way to prevent the fighter pilot from killing his own comrades was to drive him off with return fire. The fighter came in at 50 feet, spraying shots. A hail of .50-cal. slugs from the Fighting Turtles discouraged a second strafing run.

About 30 miles west of Berlin, the Sixth Armored Division received its final wartime orders and ground to a halt. Engines were killed, and the combat-hardened Fighting Turtles simply sat for two weeks. A deal had been made between Roosevelt, Stalin and Churchill. Berlin was to be taken not by the Americans and the British, who'd fought the Germans back through the Dragon's Teeth to their capital, but by the Russians, who were moving in from the east, lusting for revenge after the agony of fighting off the Germans on the Eastern Front. As the men of the Sixth sat in their tanks, Berliners—soldiers and civilians alike—flooded west out of the city to surrender to the them.

"They didn't want to surrender to the Russians," Vink

said. "They definitely didn't want to do that."

Finally, word came over the Sad Sack's radio. It had fil-
tered down from the high command to the divisions, to the
batallions, to the companies and, finally, to the platoons. The
Third Reich was no more. The war in Europe was over.

"Well," Vink recalled, "we all had a couple of drinks.
Then we just sat there, waiting for more orders. Then we got
relieved. They moved us back to Frankfurt, and we sat there
for a while. Then they moved us into a town called Ronheim,
and we had to stay there until the Russians came in and
relieved us. We gave up all that territory that we had captured
and gave it to the Russians."

The victorious American and Russian troops eyed one
another warily. One immediate source of friction was the poor
care the Russians had given the American military equipment
that had been supplied to them for their push from Mother
Russia. American troops had scrupulously maintained their
weaponry; the Russians had not. The Americans were
annoyed at the lack of professionalism they felt the Russians
displayed.

"They had rag bags on their feet," Vink said many years
later. "They had no boots. They were a ragtag army. Of
course, you've got to remember, too, that they went through
hell. You can't take that away from them. . . . But they got to
the point where they hated everybody."

Along the way, Vink and other American soldiers had
come into possession of a number of Mickey Mouse watches,
which fascinated the Russians. Despite the essential distrust
each side felt for the other, commerce quickly broke out. Vink
sold four watches for $150 apiece in invasion money.
Negotiations were conducted through sign language, smiles
and frowns. The capitalists were gleefully fleecing the communists. Vink got his buddy Eddie to commandeer a Jeep for
his final foray into the Russian camp.

"Keep it running," Vink told Eddie as he made his
deal—another $150 for still one more Mickey Mouse watch.
Vink then piled into the Jeep and urged Eddie to step on it. As

they pulled away from the Russian camp, Eddie asked what the rush was all about. Vink explained that he'd tested that final watch. It always quit after five minutes.

"We never went down to that end of the town again," Vink recalled.

After the war ended, The Sixth Armored Division was broken up. Some men, surviving veterans of combat all the way from D-Day to the edge of Berlin, were shipped home. Replacements like Vink were moved to other outfits. Transferred from the Fighting Turtles, Vink found himself and 15 other members of his original company now members of the Third Armored Division. As Vink and his crew piloted their tank to their new outfit, they found themselves moving up a mountain road of yellow brick.

"We got to the top of the mountain," Vink recalled. "It was dark. During the day, we'd seen how tanks had gone right over the side. . . . I said, 'I think we'd better pull over. We're not going down that mountain road at nighttime.' So, the next morning, it was sprinkling rain, and we had steel tracks. We got down to the bottom, and the steering lever jammed. There was a line of cars at the bottom, waiting for us to make our turn, and there was a German cop there directing traffic. Well, he gave us the signal to make a right turn, and the driver pulled the levers, and nothing happened. There was a car there. We cut it right off at the windshield with the track. I don't know where the people went. They got out somehow, and they were gone. And right across the street was a gas station. A woman was out there yelling, waving her arms, 'You can't come in here! You can't come in here!' We took the building right with us."

Later in the journey, the steering lever jammed again, and the Sherman suddenly swerved off the road. As it clanked to a stop, the heavy hatch came slamming down on Vink's hand, smashing his thumb. He spent three days at the 20th Field Hospital, where the hand underwent what was ultimately an unsatisfactory repair job. Vink could never really bend the thumb ever again. He often reflected on the irony of the injury—all those months in heavy tank combat in the Battle of the Bulge, shells falling all around him, day after day, and not a scratch. Then Doug Vink's hand was permanently injured in what was, essentially, a traffic accident.

It was a less serious version of what happened to Patton, who died of injuries sustained in a car crash in post-war Germany. Like Doug Vink, Patton hadn't cared much for the Russians, either.

Once the U.S. military settled into a post-war occupation mode, with its younger members ordered to remain in Europe while their more experienced comrades were shipped back home, Vink was transferred to an infantry unit.

"After I went to the 29th Infantry," Vink said, "I was only there a couple of days when they came around and said, 'Who would like to go to the Riviera?' So, I says, 'Oh, hell, I'll go.' I got to Nice, just down from the gambling casino. We weren't allowed to go in there in uniform. Some of the guys used to change into civilian clothes and go, but they got caught and court-martialed."

The American soldiers clever enough to avoid court martial were also clever enough to realize that spending money could be realized by selling their uniforms to the Moroccan soldiers who infested post-war Nice. Like so many others, Vink kept the uniform he was wearing and sold the others for spending money in what had been Europe's premier playground before the war. When they returned to their bases, the GI's said they'd lost their other uniforms in action. The Army knew better, of course, but it also knew better than to charge veterans of so much action for missing uniforms.

At one point, Vink met an attractive Frenchwoman in a bar. She complained that she had no shoes. Vink got her size. The next morning, he went out on the beach and picked up two pairs of women's shoes in the correct size—shoes left on the beach during midnight swims in the party atmosphere that surrounded life in post-war Nice. He returned to the bar and exchanged the shoes for a case of cognac. Back in Germany, he sold the cognac to other soldiers at his home base. Unlike the

Mickey Mouse watches, he didn't have to worry about the cognac failing to do its job.

Doug Vink got on the ship to return to the States on Christmas Day 1945. He arrived in New York on January 5, 1946, the same month he turned 21 years old. It was seven months after the frenzy of excitement that had greeted the return of soldiers who'd entered the Army earlier.

In later years, he said, "I can see why the Vietnam vets felt so bad. . . . I stopped in Times Square, and I went into one of those clothes-clean-and-press-while you wait—because I'd worn that uniform all through the war, and you know how it gets dirt around the collar and everything else like that. And I said, 'I'd like to get this cleaned and pressed while I'm here.' And the guy said, "we don't have time to fool with you people. We're busy.' And I said, 'The hell with you.'

"And I came home."

General Dwight D. Eisenhower holds pens used for the
signing of Germany's unconditional surrender
(*Associated Press Photo*)

AL COHEN

☆ ☆

When the war ended in May 1945, Al Cohen and his outfit were moved initially to an area of Germany that had served as the training ground for Rommel's Afrika Corps. Shortly thereafter, the GI's were transferred to Amberg. Suddenly, after serving as combat soldiers seeing Europe at its worst, the GI's were now seeing Europe as tourists at government expense.

With the glorious continental summer in full swing, Cohen got a 10-day pass to Switzerland. He took in Geneva and Lake Luzerne and took a boat ride on a Swiss lake. At one point, he and some buddies checked into a local hotel and decided to eat dinner in the hotel dining room. As they entered, the hotel manager approached the GI's.

"I know your country remains at war with Japan," the manager said. "There are a few Japanese people in the dining room. Please, we want no problems."

There were none. The GI's had had enough of trouble for a while. As far as they were concerned, MacArthur could take care of the Japanese, and he did. The Japanese empire surrendered in August.

When Cohen returned to Amberg, he learned that the 90th Division was being broken up. Men who'd been in combat since D-Day were going home. Early replacements, like Cohen, were being reassigned to new outfits with new duties. Some were transferred to military government outfits to serve as foot soldiers in the occupation of Germany. Some went to trucking outfits, assigned to move relief supplies to citizens of the defeated, devastated country. New replacements were en route from the States, although a move was underway in the U.S. Senate to end the draft, a sentiment that was not popular with the combat veterans. In a letter home, Cohen wrote, "All of us are boiling over about the senators wanting to stop drafting 18 and 19-year-old boys for occupation because 'they're children.' Well, [they] ought to have been here a year ago when the so-called kids fought and died so two-faced people like them could live in peace. I wonder what's wrong with the people back home—have they forgotten already?"

The U.S. Army had special plans for Al Cohen. In early October, he found himself assigned to the First Infantry Division. He was going to Nuremberg. The surviving leadership of the Nazi Party and key figures in what had been the government of the Third Reich were going on trial, charged with war crimes. They needed to be guarded. So, Al Cohen, machine gunner, was issued a white helmet and white pistol belt and began work as a prison guard.

Nuremberg had been the target of 11 Allied bombing raids in the closing months of the war. While a few buildings remained intact—including Nuremberg Prison, where prisoners were being housed, and the nearby Palace of Justice, where the trials were to be held—the city was mostly rubble. Its suburbs, however, had been largely undamaged. So, after months of sleeping first in the snow and then in the mud, Cohen now found himself sharing a cozy apartment with three other GI's on the outskirts of Nuremberg. The apartment had curtains and its own bathroom.

And no booby traps beneath the toilet seat.

With the fighting finished, soldiering was no longer a 24-hour-a-day job. Now the battle-weary GI's worked regular shifts, which left them free to find fun—a chore they worked at assiduously. To their surprise, they found German civilians generally friendly, especially the younger women, although such relationships were not without their risks. After all those months of dodging bullets and bombs, the GI's took in stride events that would have shocked them in their former civilian lives back in the U.S. At one point, Cohen wrote home, "As usual, there isn't anything exciting to write about. One of the boys in my platoon got shot in the stomach by a German girl and isn't expected to live. So it goes."

Years later, Cohen recalled, "At five o'clock in the morning, you would look out the window, and you saw all the girls leaving the apartment house that we lived in. . . . Guys would bring them home, and they were out at five o'clock in the morning, and nobody said anything. The lieutenant that we had, he'd landed at Normandy with the First Division. He was just waiting for his time to go, so he didn't care."

Cohen was assigned to the prison's main cell block. He wrote home, "Please don't get excited about the word 'prison' as I'm only doing guard duty and not time." Nuremberg Prison was commanded by no-nonsense Colonel Burton Andrus and was linked to the Palace of Justice by a walkway. It housed men who'd spent years wielding immense power inside the Third Reich. Among others behind bars were Colonel General Alfred Jodl, the slim, balding operations chief of the German armed forces; Rudolf Hess, the one-time third-ranking boss of the Nazi Party who, hoping to achieve peace with the British, had flown a plane to England in 1941 and been taken into custody there after he'd parachuted down from 20,000 feet; Wilhelm Frick, former German interior minister and author of some of the earliest laws designed to persecute Jews; Julius Streicher, publisher of *Der Sturmer*, the pro-Nazi, anti-Semitic tabloid; Grand Admiral Erich Raeder, former chief of the German navy, and Grand Admiral Karl Donitz, his successor; Hans Frank, Nazi governor-General of Poland under Hitler and a profoundly brutal man; Baldur von Schirach, creator of the Hitler Youth; Albert Speer, who'd supervised the Nazi slave labor program; Field Marshall Wilhelm Keitel, chief of staff of the German armed forces and—the proceedings' biggest fish—Hermann Goering, Hitler's number two. Goering was a World War I air ace who'd grown hugely fat and drug dependent during the last years of the Third Reich. Nonetheless, Goering remained the most powerful personality in the prison.

The guards sat in on interrogations of the prisoners. Cohen stood guard while several of them told of the German troops sent into Poland before Germany made its invasion of that country in 1939. The undercover troops were to fire on uniformed German troops to provide an excuse for the already scheduled Nazi invasion. The guards also kept careful watch on the prisoners as they sat in their cells, as they were moved from the prison to the courtroom and back, as the prisoners passed time in the walled, tree-studded courtyard between the prison and the Palace of Justice. Cohen noted that several of them—Hess, in particular—seemed totally out of touch with the reality of their surroundings. Rudolf Hess, Cohen quickly concluded, was demented.

"He had an odd look to him," Cohen recalled, "big bushy eyebrows. When he was younger, he might have been good-looking, but by then he just looked odd. The first time I took him out he had to be handcuffed to me. He had exceptionally long arms. I started walking with him, and one of my shoulders was dragged way down because he had such long arms. I figured, he's going to walk the way I want him to walk. So I yanked his arm up. After that, whenever I walked him, he would remember and hold his arm up."

The other Nazis seemed to regard Hess with the same revulsion Cohen felt for the man; they avoided contact with him. Goering, a man of serious intellect and resolve blended with immense evil at the core of his being, clearly was the dominant figure in the exercise yard. He ignored Hess, with whom he'd worked so closely for so long. In the final years of the Third Reich, Goering had become a dissolute figure, grossly overweight and addicted to paracodeine tablets. Now 70 pounds lighter, his clothing hung on him like a tent, Cohen noticed. Goering occasionally would deign to speak to the other prisoners, but he clearly expected to be executed, seemed reconciled to his fate and never lowered himself to chit-chat with the guards.

"The standing order was that you weren't supposed to talk to them," Cohen said many years later, "but whenever I went on guard, whoever I was guarding, I would tell them, 'Ich bin Juden.' The first one I did that to was Streicher. He was a little off his rocker. He used to pace back and forth in his cell and mumble to himself. But as soon as I said that to him, he'd just look at you and turn his back. Or, if he could, he'd walk away."

That was not true, however, of von Schirach, the founder of the Hitler Youth. He was a compulsively talkative man. Von Schirach asked Cohen what part of America he was from. Upstate New York, Cohen replied. As a boy, von Schirach told Cohen, he'd routinely journeyed with his mother to summer in the Catskill Mountains, about 50 miles from where Cohen had grown up. The Catskills were home to fabled resorts catering to Jews from the New York City metro area, but the mountains between New York City and Albany also had been a favorite recreational area for the *Volksbund*, known to most Americans as the Bund, a Nazi-inspired organization active in the United States in the years before the war.

For the most part, however, contact between the guards and the fallen Nazi leadership was limited, and the guards liked it that way. They did their jobs, but they performed their duties while understanding that millions had died because of the unspeakable actions of these broken, unimpressive men they were guarding at Nuremberg Prison.

"You would just look at those guys," Cohen recalled, "and all you could think of was, 'and these were the people who wanted to rule the world?'"

GI's who'd entered the military near the end of the war in Europe, as had Al Cohen, had been pledged to serve for the duration of the war, plus six months. As the Nuremberg trials dragged on through the winter of 1945-1946 and into the spring, Cohen's time was drawing near. He was asked to extend his enlistment for six more months. Were he willing to do so, he was told, he would be flown home for a month. He would then be flown back to Europe to serve out those six months as a continuing cog in the engine of justice dealing with the defeated Nazi leadership. Cohen pondered the matter. He'd struggled to get into the war, battled his way through northern Europe to see the Third Reich crumble and knew that the entire effort was now in its final stages. In the end, however, he said no.

"As I look back," he said many years later, "I should have done it. . . . I was nineteen years old. I wanted to get home. . . . At the time, it looked like the trials were going to drag on for another year."

They didn't, though. In October 1946, the Nuremberg trials ended after 315 days of proceedings. Colonel General Afred Jodl was sentenced to death. So was Wilhelm Frick, the Nazi interior minister. Hans Frank, Hitler's governor-general of Poland, also was sentenced to hang, along with Field Marshall Wilhelm Keitel. Hermann Goering, incensed at being denied the right to death by a firing squad, as he felt a soldier deserved, cheated the hangman by poisoning himself in his Nuremberg Prison cell. Erich Raeder and Karl Donitz, the naval commanders, were imprisoned, as was slave labor exploiter Albert Speer, who later emerged from prison to write a best-selling book about his adventures as a Nazi bigwig. Julius Streicher, the Jew-baiting newspaper publisher who'd been so disturbed to be guarded by a Jew, was executed. Rudolf Hess spent the rest of his life behind bars, dying at 93 in what might have been a suicide or, as some suspect, was really murder. And Baldur von Schirach, the Hitler youth creator who'd told Al Cohen of his pleasant summers in the bucolic Catskills? He was sentenced to 20 years.

Five months before the trials played out, Cohen and some buddies had managed to get permission to spend a few days at a First Division rest camp in the mountains. It was a German resort on a lake halfway up an Alp.

"If you were lucky," Cohen recalled, "you'd get a week up there. So, three of us from our company went there. In the morning, a two-and-a-half-ton truck would go down the mountain, and you could catch a ride on that in the morning and catch a ride back at night. Otherwise, you had to walk ten miles up the mountain. . . . So, we're standing in line one morning to get paid, and the company clerk says, 'Cohen, you're on orders to go home.' That's how I found out."

Cohen and other departing GI's packed up and caught a train from Nuremburg to a military installation at Le Harve, a seaport at the mouth of the Seine. There they were chargined to learn that no clerks were available to cut departure orders that would enable the GI's to board a converted freighter riding at anchor in the harbor. Cohen and a few other men could type. They scrounged up some typewriters and a mimeograph machine. They spent a night creating their own orders and mimeographing them. They then found an officer to sign them only to discover that they'd filled out the paperwork improperly. The GI's were forced to spend another night creating new orders before the officer would affix his signature to them.

Once aboard the freighter, Cohen managed to get a lower canvas bunk in the freighter's hold, which was stacked with hundreds of soldiers. His quarters were markedly less lavish than what he'd enjoyed on the *Queen Elizabeth* on his way to enter the war in Europe. Moreover, the motion of this smaller vessel on the open sea induced widespread seasickness. In short order, the ship's interior reeked of vomit. Cohen, as sick as anybody else, curled up in his bunk to wait it out. An officer came by to order him out of the bunk and out on deck.

"Leave me alone," Al Cohen told the officer dismissively. "I'm dying."

As GI's moved home to return to real life, military discipline aboard the freighter predictably eroded. Soldiers designated as MP's were supposed to enforce anti-gambling orders. Nonetheless, card games and crap games were continuous activities, night and day. Many returning GI's were going home with dogs they'd picked up in Europe. Every day the freighter's deck was alive with men strolling with their boxers or German shepherds as the vessel sliced steadily through the waves westward, toward America. The weather was blissfully sunny and warm for each of the 13 days of the voyage. Dolphins frolicked about the ship's hull.

"We pulled into New York Harbor in the morning," Cohen recalled. "Everybody ran to see the Statue of Liberty. We pulled up to a dock. They had a big 'V' painted on the dock, and two MP's standing there, and that was our welcoming committee. From there they took us to Fort Dix."

Mustering out of the Army took a few days. On a weekend afternoon, Cohen and some buddies sneaked out of camp and across the Hudson to renew their acquaintance with Manhattan. He later recalled, "We walked around Times Square, four or five of us. We were all from the Ninetieth. These guys started talking to some girls, and it was like nothing. You know, we all wore combat badges; we all had ribbons. And it was just like nothing had happened."

Back at Dix, Cohen rejected a pitch to join the reserves. He was officially separated from the U.S. Army on July 3, 1946. Now a civilian again, Al Cohen went back across the Hudson and caught a train for home. Three hours later, still in uniform, he stepped down from the train at Albany's Union Station. He sat around the station for a few moments, reflecting on what he'd seen, done and endured since he'd last been inside this huge structure. He'd wanted desperately to go to war, and he had, and now it was done. Then Al Cohen stood, gathered up his gear and went outside to walk a block and to catch a bus a dozen or so more blocks down Pearl Street to Morton Avenue.

And home.

The Nuernberg Trials

Hermann Goering

Rudolf Hess

(Associated Press Photos)

Rich Marowitz's band at the AWOL Club

RICHARD MAROWITZ

☆ ☆

With the war at an end in Europe, the possibility of being relocated to the Pacific theatre loomed large in the minds of most soldiers. The unknown of jungle fighting was much less appealing than the cold, rugged battles they had become accustomed to. The Rainbow had acquitted itself admirably— logging 114 days in combat, turning back the *Nordwind* invasion in the Alsace region against overwhelming odds, as well marching across Germany and capturing the cities of Wurzburg, Schweinfurt, Furth, Nurnberg and Munich. The Division had marched 450 miles, through the rugged Hardt Mountains, to the boarders of Austria. Along the way, they'd captured numerous villages, 51,000 prisoners and liberated the grateful souls who'd endured the horror that was Dachau. Now, as they prepared for occupation of conquered territories, they were no longer the green GI's who'd huddled in the tent city of CP 2 that first night in Europe. Months of combat had molded them into a first-class fighting unit that had done their namesake proud.

Rich Marowitz had grown along with his adolescent unit. He was now much more than the streetwise, 125-pound civilian trumpet player who'd boarded a bus for Fort Dix almost a year earlier. He'd gone from serving in the officers mess, to riding shotgun for an action-addicted captain, to serving as a point man for a fighting division that had made its mark on history. Fitting into the European occupation regime—or boarding a boat to fight on the other side of the world—lay ahead, but one mission still remained for Marowitz and the I and R platoon.

The Rainbow's initial occupation assignment was in the town of Tyrol, a peaceful slice of beautiful picturesque countryside highlighted by rugged mountains. Many German soldiers and SS troops reportedly had fled into the Tyrolean Alps to escape capture and possible trial on war crimes charges. Two weeks after the war in Europe officially ended, the I and R platoon was called to headquarters and assigned a Tyrolean guide. They were ordered to go up in the mountains and search for Wehrmacht, some of whom may not have been aware the war had ended.

"We were supposed to go and break up weapons, radios, equipment or anything else we found up there," Marowitz remembered, "which was pretty stupid. You know how long it takes to climb a mountain? The guy could be standing up there laughing and be three mountains away by the time you got there. We did find some huts and broke up some communications and a couple of weapons. It was just a dumb mission."

The technique of combing the mountains to round up prisoners was not very effective, although a few isolated arrests were made—including that of SS General Carl Oberg, known as the "Butcher of Paris." He was captured by another Rainbow patrol in a ski lodge high above the tree line. The most productive means of capturing Nazis, however, was by setting up roadblocks every few kilometers and requiring local citizens to carry passes. In the towns, a screening process was established by interrogating everyone in the area. Possible hideouts were investigated again and again. The systematic casting of this smothering net eventually wore down many fugitives who'd eluded the conquerors temporarily but eventually accepted the futility of their effort and surrendered to the Americans.

On May 23rd, a training program was instituted to prepare the Rainbow for jungle combat. Instruction in Japanese fighting techniques, range firing and physical conditioning were emphasized. Unbeknownst to the men of the Rainbow Division, a deployment to the Pacific was not in their future. On August 5th, the U.S. would drop the atomic bomb on Hiroshima. Nine days later the Japanese would surrender.

Early in July, the Rainbow was reassigned from Tyrol to Salzburg. The GI's hated to leave the spacious, peaceful environs of Tyrol for Salzburg, which was jammed with troops and refugees. Some Rainbow men would have to move back into tents until the 101st Airborne was redeployed. The inconvenience was short-lived. A month later, the 222nd Regiment was shipped to Vienna to serve as part of a four-nation military government contingent that included Russia, Britain and France. The division would serve as honor-company for General Mark W. Clark. By August 27th, all 222nd units were in place to garrison the city and serve as a peacekeeping occupation force for Austria.

Vienna was divided into four quadrants with each of the four nations in charge of a specific area. Marowitz found the British and French quadrants congenial, but the Russian section was another matter. He found it easy to understand why the Germans had been terrified of falling under Russian control. The Russians were a rough bunch who hated Germans because of the Nazi atrocities perpetrated on the eastern front. The Russians were conspicuous among the Allied occupiers for their harsh handling of the citizenry.

To travel into any of the three quadrants not controlled by his nation, an American soldier needed a pass written in French, English and Russian. On one occasion, Marowitz's mother contacted him and asked him to deliver a package to the daughter of a friend who operated a candy store back in Brooklyn. Marowitz agreed to deliver the package but had second thoughts after discovering that the address was in the Russian zone.

"The Russians had a lot of these Mongolian guys," he recalled. "They were all pock-marked and nasty. We used to find dead women behind our Red Cross, and rumor had it that they were responsible. Once I received the package and asked where it [the address] was, that's when I found out it was in the Russian sector. They would tell me how to get there, but no one would go with me. Nobody wanted to deal with the Russians. Finally, a buddy of mine agreed to go. We went sneaking around in there until we found the building. There were no lights, so I had to use a Zippo lighter to find the apartment number. I knocked, and a heavy, German-accented guy answered. I said I had a package, and the door cracked open and a huge guy with a gun answered. Once they saw what we had, they treated us like cousins. We decided it was best to get out while it was still dark. We got shot at two or three times and got chased. Finally we had to hide out at a lady's house that had rooms to rent. We slept for two hours and then got the hell out of there. I wrote my mother and told her, 'No more packages.'"

Once settled in Vienna, some Rainbow men were chosen to pursue college courses made available by the Army. They worked on their studies around tasks that included feeding displaced persons, guarding national treasures and military installations and—in the case of Rich Marowitz—playing the trumpet in a band that he assembled. Recreation became a command priority in helping the warriors adjust both to the boredom of occupation duty and to what would soon be a return to civilian life. Warfare behind them, they involved themselves in division football teams, track teams, baseball teams. They frequented libraries, movies and clubs. It was also possible for the GI's to cable wives and family members regularly—even to send flowers.

Marowitz had been called into the Command Post by the lieutenant in charge of special services and assigned a two-and-a-half-ton truck and a driver. He was told to put a band together and venture out to the surrounding towns and entertain the troops stationed there. Marowitz was handed a map to show him where the troops were located. Soon he was on the road with his new band.

Marowitz recalled, "We had this guy named Pappy

who played the bass fiddle. He really couldn't play; he just kind of slapped at it. He had false teeth. He used to take out his teeth while he was playing. The guys really got a kick out of it. We also had this kid that sang, but he only knew one song. After a few weeks I told him if he didn't learn another song I was going to kill him. I played trumpet and told a few jokes. It wasn't great entertainment, but the guys liked it, and it was better than nothing."

In September, some veteran Rainbow men had earned enough points to go home. The Rainbow ended up absorbing 5,000 low-point men from the 66th Infantry Division. The arrival and departure of soldiers gave Marowitz an opportunity to upgrade his band, which ultimately became recognized as the best in all of Austria.

"Eventually we had four saxophones, three trumpets, one trombone, a drum, piano and bass," Marowitz said decades later. "We had a 12-piece orchestra. My brother was with the Harry James band back home, and he was sending me great arrangements. Rich Fish was our piano player and a Julliard student. He was from the Bronx and a great technical pianist, but he was stiff as a board. I told him, 'You gotta loosen up a little 'cause this is swing.' He had a great musical mind and ended up writing some arrangements for us."

With the occupation now becoming routine, entertainment blossomed. Small clubs started popping up around Vienna, thanks in large part to the U.S. Army. Interdivision competition developed in all levels of sporting events. Bands were no different. Marowitz's band was the envy of many as the musicians opened up the swankiest nightclub in town in what had been a classy coffee house. Crystal chandeliers hung from the ceiling. The club was open only to enlisted men and their dates—no officers allowed. Nightly, until 2 AM, Marowitz's musicians belted out big-band concerts bolstered by the best singer in the armed forces, Jimmy Roselli.

"When Jimmy got back to the states to continue his career," Marowitz recalled, "he developed a reputation as a great singer of Italian songs. I heard a rumor that Frank

Sinatra called him to sing at his mother's birthday party, but they got in an argument over money and Frank had him black balled. If it's true, I guess you don't argue with Frank Sinatra over money."

His time in Austria was not all sweet melodies for Marowitz. At one point he had to be hospitalized for six weeks with an ankle infection. He found, however, that the hospital was a great place in which to meet new friends.

"The place was filled with all these pretty nurses," Marowitz recalled. "After my first night, the next morning this cute little thing comes in with a sponge and water basin. She said, 'How would you like to do this?' I told her, 'You wash down as far as possible, and then wash up as far as possible. And then leave 'Possible' to me.' She laughed. They were a lot of fun, I became friends with all of them."

For the enlisted men, the Christmas ball in Vienna was the premiere event of 1945. Two thousand couples were expected to attend, and the event was to be broadcast back to the States on Armed Forces Radio. No expense was to be spared. Marowitz and his band were playing at their nightclub when the regiment commander, Colonel Henry L. Luongo— with General Mark Clark in tow—paid them a visit. The colonel explained that he and General Clark had been listening to all the bands in Austria to select one to play at the Christmas gala. They wanted to hear Marowitz's band. Marowitz assured the officers that he and his musicians would do their best. Then he informed his musicians.

"I was so shook up, I didn't say anything else," Marowitz recalled. "I told the band, 'No clinkers tonight, guys.' They asked what was up, and I told them. All of a sudden one of our bouncers came over and tapped me on the shoulder. He said, 'The colonel wants you to play his favorite song.' I said, 'Sure. What is it?' He said, 'The colonel said you know what it is.' I said, 'How the hell am I supposed to know what it is? Did I ever dance with him?' Now the guys in the band were nervous and wanted to know what we should do. I said everybody likes Stardust; play that. And we did. The bouncer comes back over and said, 'The colonel said that's just the way he likes it.' The guys said, 'You did it again.' I figured what's he gonna do if I was wrong—hang me? He must have liked it, because we did get chosen to play at the ball."

Some of the gratification involved in being part of Army entertainment during the occupation was diminished by the instruments available. Marowitz always had his own mouthpiece, but the only horn he could find in Vienna he later characterized as a "Czechoslovakian pea shooter"—a long skinny, small-bore instrument he found difficult to play. To get anything close to the sound he desired, he was overblowing the instrument. By the end of a night of playing, he was suffering pain all through his diaphragm, sometimes so severe that he had trouble remaining on his feet. He soon abandoned the pea shooter and tried to work with a flugle horn. It had rotary valves like a French horn. He struck up a conversation about his instrument problem with some Army Air Corps pilots at the Red Cross. One of the pilots played a little trumpet. They informed Marowitz that the Selmer factory had reopened in Paris. He immediately went off to find a guy he knew in the drum and bugle corps who'd just gotten a weekend pass to Paris.

"Selmer was one of the top horns in the world at that time," Marowitz recalled. "So I told the guy to go and buy me a horn—any B-flat trumpet; it didn't matter. I'd pay for it. Just before the war they came out with the balance model. It was called that because is was longer with the valves in the middle. It had great sound. It was so great that you could use it for a symphony, but it still had the brilliance for a dance club. He said okay, and when I heard he got back I went to see him. He took out this cardboard box with the trumpet in it. It was the balance model, and it was heavy, but it was all out of tune. I didn't care. So, I said, 'What do I owe you?' He said, 'I only could get one, and I'm going to keep it.' Well, I started making him offers, everything under the sun. Finally he said, 'I guess I pulled your chain long enough.' And he reached under the bed and pulled out another box. I picked up the trumpet and played it. This one was in perfect tune. It was a good thing he didn't know his ass from a hole in the ground when it came to sound.

"The horn wasn't lacquered, and the valves weren't plated, and the only engraving was the Selmer logo. I carried it home with me and took it to the Bach factory and had it gold plated and engraved. I still have it under my bed with another horn my brother bought me. I don't play either one any more."

The junior officers were annoyed that the best band in the area belonged to the enlisted men. The officers had a German band that would often come by the club begging for instructions from Marowitz and his colleagues on how they could sound more like the Americans. Somehow, though, the German band never sounded quite as good as the enlisted men's band. On certain special occasions Marowitz's band would agree to play for the officers.

"One night," he recalled, "we'd agreed to play at the officers club. So, who do I see dancing with the officers but all the nurses who took care of me while I was in the hospital with my infected ankle. So, they all gather round me, and I'm rocking. A special services officer, a lieutenant, walks over and says, 'Rich, you work for me, and you put a great band together. You do the entertaining, and I like you, but right now all those officers hate your guts because they want to be dancing with these nurses.' I turned to the nurses, and I said, 'Did you hear that? You better go dance with those crappy little guys over there.' They were really mad."

While in Vienna, Marowitz was offered several opportunities for advancement in the Army, but with soldiers on their way home most of the other good bands were breaking up. Marowitz soon found himself with a musical monopoly. The nightclub was going strong. The band played. Jimmy Roselli sang. During intermission, Marowitz told jokes, and waiters in tuxedos took care of the patrons. It was a very classy set-up, and while no one involved collected a dime beyond his Army salary, other chances to earn a buck came along. For example, a particular air base just outside Vienna lacked its own band.

"Most of the pilots were colonels and majors," Marowitz said many years later, "but they looked like a bunch of babies. They had lots of money. We'd get done at 2 AM, and they'd send over a truck to pick us up, and we'd go to the base and play 'til five. They'd give us a great steak dinner, all the booze we could drink, pay us well and then take us back home. We'd sleep all day till it was time to go back the next night.

"We played with the Red Cross and also on this showboat that went up and down the Danube River. We got paid for all of it. We got this new sergeant, and he was always after me to take a promotion, but I didn't want it. I would have had other duties and have to cut back with the band. He would always be at me, saying, 'How can you pass up the money?' Finally, I had to tell him what was going on. He said, 'I figured you were up to something.' But he never said anything to anyone. He was a great guy. We had a really good thing going."

In June 1946, that "really good thing"—among all the really bad things that define war—came to an end. Rich Marowitz was shipped home. His talent for entertaining went with him, and his return journey to the U.S. was not at all unlike the voyage that had taken him to France 18 months earlier.

"When we got on the ship coming home, it stormed all the way," Marowitz recalled as he neared 80 years of age. "Guys were sick all over the place. It was like a cork in water. One of the officers asked if anyone could put something together. So, Ziggy, another trumpet player, Jimmy Roselli and I and another guy from New York put a show together called 'Anything Goes.' We had to do it a number of times so the whole ship could see it. I still have the ship's newspaper with it in it—everybody's names and all. It's yellow now, though."

☆ ☆ ☆ ☆ ☆

After the war, Al Cohen went to work in the sporting goods business as a clerk and a buyer. He married Jean Pearlman, to whom he'd written from Europe. Doug Vink married Ann Welch and spent his working life as a foreman for a utility company. Rich Marowitz watched popular music change and didn't like the changes. His lust for life on the road faded. He moved from Brooklyn to Albany, became a manufacturer of coats for women and children and married Ruth Bosworth. The post-war lives of the warriors filled up with work — and with children, grandchildren and great-grandchildren.

Adolf Hitler's top hat made its way from Europe to America in Rich Marowitz's duffel bag. The hat later spent some time in the National Museum of American Jewish Military History in Washington. It also became the subject of a documentary, "Hitler's Hat," by independent filmmaker Jeff Krulik.

Vink, Cohen and Marowitz had been three among a million who'd fought in the Battle of the Bulge. They hadn't known one another then. It was not until decades later that they met as retirees and as members of a veterans group. With some time on their hands at long last, they discerned a new duty — to play useful roles in helping young people understand what the world had been like when they'd been young and when humanity had faced its greatest threat ever to civilized values.

The presentation at Niskayuna High School is winding down now. Vink, Cohen and Marowitz are taking questions from the high school kids, and answering them as best they can. They're waiting for the question that always comes, sooner or later. Finally, one of the students asks it.

"How many Nazis did you guys kill?"

This time, it's Marowitz who fields the inevitable inquiry.

"There is absolutely no way of knowing," he says, "and if anybody gives you the exact number of how many they killed, he's probably yanking your chain. Let me explain: Most of the time, you're firing covering fire so your fellow soldiers can get up to where the enemy is. And when you get up there and find a lot of dead Germans, nobody knows who hit who."

The kids won't let it go. Another asks, "Which one do you think, out of all of you, killed the most Nazis?"

"There's no way of knowing," Marowitz says.

"Half the time you don't see them," Vink explains.

A girl asks, "Did you guys ever have any problems with friendly fire?"

Marowitz shrugs. "All the time."

The bell sounds. Marowitz thanks the students for their attention. After delivering a round of applause, the teenagers file out, on their way to the next class. Cohen, Vink and Marowitz sit behind the table, watching them go. A questioner remains, however, and asks: "Why do you come and speak at the schools? What's the real reason for coming and doing this?"

Marowitz says, "For me, the real reason is to educate those who are most important. That's the kids. . . . Somebody has to let them know what went on."

Cohen says, "You know, when we went in, it was the tail end of the Depression, and you didn't argue with anyone. Patriotism was there. But since World War II, there hasn't been any patriotism. In schools, they're fighting about the Pledge of Allegiance. They don't like the wording of it. . . . When we started out, that was the one thing we wanted to bring out. . . . One of the good things about this country is that you can demonstrate. You can be for it or against it, and nobody will lock you up for it."

Vink says, "If we don't do it, who's going to? These kids are missing valuable lessons if fellows like ourselves—and future generations—don't come out and speak about the wars, and let them know just what it was about and the reasons for it. We didn't just go to war 'cause we wanted to fight."

Then it's over. The aged men in dated Army uniforms

gather up their gear—the Nazi flag, the photos and maps, the mess kits, Hitler's hat—and move out into the school's parking lot. They have had their parades. Now, they leave the building without fuss, without fanfare—three of the dwindling number of living monuments to the quiet, workaday valor of a crueler, more perilous era. At a time when they should have been enjoying the pleasures of adolescence, they'd instead risked their lives on a frozen, bloody battlefield forever emblazoned in the annals of history. Now, they leave this school building quietly. They bear with them both their presentation material and their pride in being among those who served and sacrificed—among the men and women who'd played such gallant roles in the dark, dangerous, defining moments of the 20th Century. A shimmering shower of sunlight glints off the snow outside the high school.

For the dead of winter, it's a glorious day.